CONTENTS

RUNNIN' WITH THE BIG DOGS

JANE GETZ

Janiac Music

Runnin' With the Big Dogs
Jane Getz

Published by Janiac Music
323-656-7939
2janiac@sbcglobal.net

Cover design, interior page layout & eBook conversions by the Ink Studio
Original cover artwork by Chloé Mathiez

ISBN: 978-0-9905500-2-0 (Trade Paperback)
ISBN: 978-0-9905500-0-6 (Kindle eBook)
ISBN: 978-0-9905500-1-3 (iPad/Nook/Kobo eBook)

Printed in the United States of America.

FOREWORD

I fell for her immediately. She just totally knocked my socks off.

It was in the seventies, and I'd answered an ad that she'd put in *Rolling Stone* for a pedal steel guitar player. It was an important gig for me. I'd been playing my new instrument (I'd played guitar since age 12) for a little less than a year, and now I had to audition for someone who had a new record out on a major label.

The album was "Mother Hen," and the girl who sang in the high fluttery voice and played the hell out of gospel/country and rock licks that were the "stuff" of her music (all original tunes) put me flat on my ass.

All I have of that first night auditioning for Jane Getz are those first few images — a tiny little girl with an amazingly beautiful body, porcelain doll-like face, and tiny hands that somehow managed to knock out some of the biggest, fattest chords I'd ever heard.

I loved *her* music right away. What's more I loved her. That was the bitch of it. The chick had me by the *cojones* — no two ways about it. She was — in my mind anyway — a star. For those of us who'd been making our living playing club gigs, anybody who had a *real* record deal — was *already* a star.

When the night was over, she went and plunked herself down in a big overstuffed chair and wiped the sweat from her brow. She hadn't been particularly friendly when I'd walked into the room, and — after an hour and a half of rehearsal — she still wasn't falling all over herself to be friendly...or even nice.

In fact, I thought to myself, as I hauled my pedal steel out to my car, she'd been kind of a bitch.

The next rehearsal didn't go much better. She kept stopping me and telling me I wasn't playing the "right stuff."

Before the night was over, I knew what was coming.

"Look," she said, as I packed up my steel... "you're a good little player, but I just don't think what you're doing works with my music."

I felt my heart sink. I pretty much knew up front that I wasn't gonna land the gig. Damn...and I'd been THAT close to landing a job with this beautiful chick with a real record deal and...and...

If I had known who "Mother Hen" really was when I'd gone into that rehearsal, I'd have been a helluva lot more intimidated than simply having a mild case of the heebie jeebies.

Just before landing the six-figure, two-album deal that had found her back in her old stomping ground of L.A. Jane Getz had been one of the most in demand pianists on the jazz circuit in and around New York.

This beautiful girl had shared the stage with some of the more major forces on the jazz scene. To name only a few — she'd toured and recorded with some of the world's greatest jazz players. Those included the likes of Charles Lloyd, Stan (No Relation) Getz, Charles Mingus, Georgie Braith, and Pony Poindexter.

"I was never intimidated," Jane recalls, thinking back now to some of the people who she worked with. "I was good, all I had to do was prove it."

For five years, Jane ran with the Big Dogs....traveling and recording with some of jazz's legends, at some of jazz's hippest spots.

But Jane wasn't about to be stuffed into a cubbyhole — be it the country music she'd grown up on....or the jazz with which she'd made her living in New York.

A musician is a musician is a musician. You can't label them. As a child whose mother trotted her out to play recitals for some of the upper-crust families in and around the Hancock Park area of L.A., she soaked it all up. Classical, jazz, gospel, R&B, rock 'n' roll. You name it — she could play it.

Moreover, Jane wasn't limited to just playing. She had a facility with words, and was writing original music from the word go. "I have an affinity for words," she recalls. "I can't really say that much about it. It's just a gift God gave me. I try to give Him back the energy — the art...whatever you want to call it — every time I sit down to write a new song.

Jane steps out onto the sun-blanched patio of her Hollywood Hills home, sipping on a cup of coffee. Every day, she walks the 30 or so steps down to the state-of-the-art recording studio.

Jane's a very busy lady. She and her partner Bob Tucker formed Janiac Music which features original songs and tracks complete with production for a variety of recording artists... and she goes nonstop...writing, coaching, and producing new artists — people who are trying to get their songs heard on the radio and on CD — from morning till night.

"I feel like I'm still learning" every day, Jane smiles. "Some of these kids (and she doesn't use the term condescendingly) are so talented....but this business is a bitch.

I try to give them what knowledge I can...but I certainly don't have the power to turn anybody into a star.

When she's asked what she loves best, she stops and thinks for a moment. "I guess I'd have to say that it'd be writing. I told you before that I have a love affair with words, and that's really true. They just seem to flow into my head — sometimes they have music with them...sometimes they don't."

"I'm always working on something," she says, replenishing her cup of coffee. "I meditate every day," she says. "It's healing...and it's also my way of thanking God for the gifts He's given me."

"Yikes!" Jane says, glancing at her watch. "I'm late for my workout." And with that, she's grabbing her purse and loping down the stairs to where her car is parked on the windy Hollywood street.

Tonight, she'll be sharing the stage with her long time pal, sax player Dale Fielder and his quintet. (Getz has recorded ten plus CD's with Fielder). Tomorrow morning, she'll be meeting a singer-songwriter, who's hoping that Jane will take her on as client.

It's almost trite to say that I'm in awe of Jane. But it's true. I love her today just as much as I did when I walked into her tiny Studio City apartment 30 years ago. In a life where friends are here one moment and gone the next, she's been there for me every day — and in every way — since the day we met.

I'm proud to say that Jane has just penned the introduction to my new book. And just like I knew she would, she found just the right words to describe my first collection of stories — which encompass over 40 years of writing and publishing in the City Of The Angels.

It's been a long road since the seventies. And we've walked a lot of miles together. In 1995, I was fortunate enough to co-produce her jazz CD, "No Relation," which her partner Bob Tucker recently re-mastered.

I don't know how else to put it. I've always been just a little bit in awe of Jane. There are a lot of genuinely gifted people in the music business, but Jane's just got something, well — extra special. She knows it...and she doesn't mince words when talking about it.

"God gave me a gift"— she says. "I wake up each morning with my eyes wide open — not knowing where the next turn in the road is going to take me. As long as I stay out of my own way, I never get too worried where I'm going to wind up. So far, it's been a great adventure," she smiles — and I just trust God that He's going to keep showing me which path to take. I know that if I stick to that pattern — and it's something you've got to practice religiously — that everything will work out the way it's supposed to.

– Stuart Goldman

RUNNIN' WITH THE BIG DOGS

*"If you want to be a politician,
go to Washington. If you want to be
a musician, go to New York."*

— Anonymous

The noonday sun was starting to turn the city into a furnace as I boarded the Greyhound. It was San Francisco in the mid sixties. I was sixteen, carrying a fake I.D., five hundred bucks, and a motherlode of hope. I saw no reason to wait. I knew what I wanted to do. For that I didn't need a high school diploma or an education.

Back then, I had only one desire, one goal: to be a legit player on the jazz scene. I'd paid enough dues playing piano around L.A. and San Francisco, so I was taking the big leap.

New York.

It was time to test the waters.

++++

Approximately three days after motoring across the Bay Bridge, the Greyhound glided through the Holland Tunnel. I looked out of the window as it headed for Port Authority. Wow! A place I never dreamed existed.

The old ivy covered brownstones, many of which had steps leading down to tiny basement apartments, were connected. Everything was touching everything else. Even the people, who were scrambling like little ants were elbowing, jostling, and sideswiping each other. And the smell! There was a sweet fruity kind of rubbery odor with a hint of smoke wafting through the city.

As the bus bounced over the potholes, I could feel the kinetic energy engulfing me. *Damn.* This was *it!* The Big Apple. The jazz Mecca. New York, New York. So hip they had to name it twice!

++++

Disembarking from the huge sputtering Greyhound, it hit me. I was actually here — bag and baggage.

I took a deep breath, walked out of Port Authority, and hailed a cab, giving the driver a piece of paper with the name of a hotel scribbled on it. He nodded and immediately went zooming down the old pitted New York streets, honking and cursing out the other drivers. We finally stopped at a residence that was infamous on the jazz scene: the Alvin Hotel. An old dilapidated building full of whirring fans and junkies, where drug deals were going down 24/7.

The first night at the Alvin, it was hard to sleep, what with all the loud whispering going on outside my door. But I finally tuned it out. I was in New York for one purpose and one purpose only — *to run with the Big Dogs.* To do that I'd have to become at least a mid-sized Dog myself. Though there *were* people that thought I was a genius, I now wondered if I really had my shit together. And even if I did, would the cats in the Big Apple accept a skinny little 5ft. 2in. white chick with kinky brown hair and green eyes as one of them?

The third day after my arrival I got my answer. Yeah, I hit paydirt. Walking through the lobby of the Alvin, I happened to glance into a phone-booth near the front desk. Inside the enclosure was an alto player I'd once jammed with in San Francisco. His name was Pony Poindexter. He was just starting to dial a number.

I rapped on the glass.

"Pony! Hey man. It's me Jane."

Pony hung up the phone and opened the creaky glass door to give me a big hug.

"Wow baby, I was just callin' Cedar Walton." As he looked me over, a light went on in his eyes. "Hey, maybe *you* can make this gig with me."

Damn! I had scored! First time outta the box! Open Sesame! My little size five foot was in the door.

This was a real opportunity and I was going to jump on that sucker full force. The gig didn't pay much, but at that point I didn't care. Maybe Pony wasn't Miles Davis or Wayne Shorter, but the cat *could* play, and better yet, he was always working.

A few days later I found myself in Pittsburgh, onstage with the Pony Poindexter quartet. The club put us up in a hotel that was situated in a hilly old section of town. From my fifth floor window I could see a warren of narrow cobblestone streets, turn-of-the-century street lamps, and ornate brick buildings. Was I in one of the Thirteen Colonies? Except for the presence of the cars and telephone poles, I felt like I had stepped into some kind of time warp.

This was nothing like Southern California — home of the carefree, blond, suntanned, surfing, pool-in-the-back-yard, necking with the top down on Mulholland types. As far as I was concerned So. Cal. was a scary place. All those rays could fry your brain and lull you into oblivion.

A week later the four of us hit Boston. We wound around the downtown area, a labyrinthine collection of old stone roadways, searching for our hotel. We did one night at some Irish bar and witnessed a mandatory barroom brawl. Then we headed for New Bedford — a town full of fishermen, souped up cars, and sober looking people who spoke Portuguese. This was a different America from the one I had grown up in.

Traveling with a band was a gas.

Our *mode* of travel was another matter.

Pony had decided, in order to save money, he'd drive us to our gigs in this old wood-paneled station wagon he'd borrowed from a buddy.

There we were, four of us and our gear, crammed like rats inside this ancient gas guzzler, tooling up and down the East coast. It was amazing that no one freaked out or had a major temper tantrum, but there was an unspoken agreement that the music was more important than our little creature comforts. *Almost....*

Pony Poindexter was altogether another trip. He either blabbed non-stop about the sorry state of his finances or, for a change of pace, maiming or killing all the ofays (white folks) in the world. At first I was very uncomfortable — not only about the subject matter, but about what stance I should take. I mean, if I was a bonafide member of his band, was I still an ofay or was I truly one of the brothers? Or maybe a band had a group identity.

Then I had a flash. I hadn't really seen Pony maim or kill anyone personally, so what the hell — he was probably just mouthing off. Besides that, I knew his whole book now, had all the tunes memorized so it would be a hassle for him to get a piano player closer to his specifications.

After awhile, I knew Pony's little routine wasn't personal, so when the cat got into his rap, I spaced out or read a magazine until I fell asleep.

++++

After New Bedford the band went back to New York. We had a few weeks off, so I went apartment hunting. I'd been to a couple of cribs uptown I liked, so I chose the Upper West Side as my designated search area.

After inspecting a bunch of hole-in-the-wall apartments with fallen plaster, chipped paint, rusted pipes, and ancient yellow crusted tubs and toilets, I finally found one that was halfway decent. Yeah, I had to pay a few bucks more, but Pony assured me he had a lot of prime gigs coming up. I was taking it on faith.

I now had a three room crib on 91st between Amsterdam and Central Park West — Spanish Harlem. As far as New York apartments went, it was quite large. The living room was a big square box, with splintering hardwood floors and one floor-to-ceiling window looking over the back alley. The middle room was small, but if I considered it a dressing room/closet, it would be ample.

The bedroom was a big rectangle and looked out on the street. It was actually the first room in a straight line of three rooms but since the entrance to the apartment was down an outside hallway that connected with the back room, the back room was actually considered the front room or living room.

Off to the side — the left hand corner to be exact — were the kitchen and bathroom. Together they were smaller than the tiny middle room. But a small kitchen didn't bother me. I'd never learned how to cook, so I just used the fridge as a storage unit for stuff from the deli.

Before I moved in, I bought a piano and a day-bed from the Salvation Army. Scouting around the neighborhood, I found an old castoff threadbare Persian rug rolled up on the curb waiting to be be picked up by the garbage collector.

I carted it up to my crib.

It was a start.

Soon, I discovered I had an upstairs neighbor by the name of Jerome Richardson — who besides being one of the heavies on the jazz scene — did lots of studio work.

One day Jerome came downstairs, welcomed me to the building and invited me up to his pad. I was completely floored. I stood there in awe. Jerome had what I considered to be just about the hippest thing ever: *adult furniture*. I didn't know anybody that owned a couch, let alone a couch that didn't have the stuffing coming out of it. Even cooler, Jerome had real pots and pans, matching silverware, and carpeting throughout. I thought of *my* floors all splintery and scuffed up .... Now *this* cat had his shit together.

Sometimes I would run into Jerome siting on the front stoop. He would always smile and ask if I was getting enough gigs, then promise he'd keep me in mind if anything came up. I thought he was just jiving me, so I was surprised when he actually came through.

"Guess what?" he said one Monday morning, inviting himself in and sitting down on my Salvation Army couch/bed.

"What?"

"I think I got you the gig with Charlie Mingus. I just talked to the cat on the phone. He'll be calling you in a couple of minutes. Don't go anywhere, baby."

Before I could even give him some show of thanks, he was in the wind. As he bounded up the stairs to his crib, a giant wave of fear rolled over me. I felt like a deer, frozen in the headlights.

Charlie Mingus. Damn! That cat was one *huge* Dog. Then I started to wonder: was I burnin' enough for that gig? Maybe I thought I was better than I actually *was?* Maybe I was a musical imposter. At that moment, I felt like a beautifully made-up ugly chick who knows how to look at herself in the mirror from just the right angle. Someone adept at the art of self-delusion, whose cover was about to be blown.

I sat there in a state of anxiety for about forty minutes. Then the phone rang.

"Hello," I answered.

"Hi is this Jane?"

It was the Big Dog himself.

"Yeah."

"Well this is Charles Mingus. Jerome Richardson gave me your number. I've got a gig in San Francisco tomorrow night. Can you make it? I got about twenty tunes to show you. Yeah, come over in maybe say... an hour?"

The next moment, Mingus was rattling off his address to me.

I looked at my watch. It would be tight but I could do it. Damn! It was one-thirty now. I could make it from Ninetieth to Twentieth by two-thirty. I was already lacing up my boots as the conversation ended.

"I'll be there," I said cementing the deal.

"Later." The Super Nova at the other end hung up.

I put down the phone, ran over to my old upright piano, and reeled off a few frantic scales. Then I went into the kitchen, grabbed a banana and bounded out the door to the subway station. I was running so fast, it almost seemed as if the wind was propelling my feet.

I felt hot and clammy as I rode down to Mingus' pad. When the train stopped at Twenty-First street, I bolted up the subway stairs and sprinted the three blocks to Mingus' crib. It was a well-kept white three-story building with trees in front of it. Cool pad. I pushed the buzzer.

Mingus buzzed me in and I took the elevator to the second floor. I'd tried to meditate during the subway ride but it didn't help. I was freaked — zoned out.

I stepped out of the claustrophobic little box trying to orient myself. Then I saw him, standing in a doorway. Mingus was a few feet away from the elevator, waving. I looked, then I looked again. *Wow!*

The word that came to mind was: Booming!! This cat was booming. His voice, his essence, his appearance, his entire being!

This was one hell of a Big Dog.

Barely acknowledging my presence, Mingus ushered me in and sat me down at his piano. Then without further ado, he got out his music. *He* was beyond any social amenities.

I quickly realized that the music itself wasn't all that hard. It was the interpretation of his music that was difficult.

"Play it like the Duke," Mingus ordered.

Being a musical child of the sixties, I didn't know what the hell he was talking about. I was into Trane, Sonny, Wayne, Miles — the cats. Not wanting to seem musically illiterate, I nodded, trying to imitate the knowing look I'd once seen Miles give Red Garland.

After running through his book, Mingus abruptly dismissed me, giving me my marching orders. I was to meet him in front of his crib tomorrow morning, eleven sharp, bags packed, ready to go. After this exchange, Mingus casually strolled into the other room and started dialing the phone.

I saw myself out.

I tried to sleep that night, but my brain was spinning with snatches of melodies and chord patterns. I finally fell asleep from sheer mental exhaustion, only to be awakened a few hours later.

Hearing the familiar buzzing sound, I flung the covers back, jumped in the shower, fed my face, did a cursory check of my bags, and ran, arms loaded to capacity, out the door.

As I flagged down a cab, I said a silent prayer asking for God's help and protection. I mean you never really know when you're going to need some roadside emergency service from the Biggest Dog ever.

When I got to Mingus' crib, his door was partially open. He was barking orders to his wife, a sweet looking young woman who Charlie told me was a nurse.

In those days there were quite a few musicians married to nurses. I wondered what significance this had? Did all these Big Dogs need around-the-clock care, or more practically, did their wives, being working professionals, guarantee a steady cash flow?

A few minutes later the rest of the band straggled in. I met Clifford Jordan (all business) and Danny Richmond who seemed warm and friendly. Danny was looking quite dapper for a guy who had a heavy rep as a junkie. Yeah, this cat was wearing the hippest threads I'd ever seen. Damn! Maybe he was a *conscientious* junkie.

In fact, Danny was the first one to see the limo pull up. Before I could grab my suitcase — which was overpacked, bulky and unwieldy — Danny grabbed it. In a show of courtliness he put it in the trunk of the limo.

The rest of the guys loaded up and we zoomed out to La Guardia, checked our bags, and boarded the big, wide TWA bird.

Not having flown such a long distance before, I was pretty nervous. Mingus, noticing my anxiety, motioned me over to sit by him. The dude could be quite intuitive.

I sat on the aisle, Mingus sat in the middle and another friend/employee of his (who was there to take care of all Charlie's needs) sat next to the window. When Charlie barked, this dude rolled over.

After take-off, Mingus, (not liking to be restrained in any manner) quickly unbuckled his seat belt. The Big Dog seemed to be in an affable mood.

About two hours into the trip, Mingus showed me something amazing. After asking his dude-in-waiting to hand him his briefcase (a kind of brown leather dossier), he casually opened it. The case contained hundreds of small bottles, each one filled with a different prescription drug. These vials weren't rattling around randomly. No sir, each bottle was held in place by a taut elastic band stretched horizontally across the length of the briefcase and attached at the sides. Charlie's Little Helpers were all labeled and completely accessible. I'd never seen anyone with such an organized addiction.

Mingus requested a glass of water from the stewardess and in one gulp downed about fifteen pills of assorted sizes and colors. Then he ordered a rare filet mignon. After the bloody repast came, he proceeded — between mouthfuls — to espouse the merits of being a vegetarian.

One thing led to another and soon he was telling me about the Vendanta Society, a meditation group founded by a Guru named Ramakrishna. The Big Dog said he was a follower of a Guru named Vivekananda, an eccentric disciple of Ramakrishna who came to America in the early 1900's and established the Vendanta Society. Vivekananda — a rebel even among yogis — wore a turban with western style clothing and smoked a pipe.

Mingus was on a roll. The cat enjoyed talking metaphysics. But as Mingus was describing the Vendanta Society's ashram in the San Bernardino mountains, a strange feeling came over me.

Suddenly, I remembered visiting an ashram in the San Bernardino mountains with my mother when I was a little child. I flashed on one of the Sisters, a tall stately blonde who played violin and lived in an A-frame house surrounded by a grove of trees. I could almost see her in her long flowing white robes giving us a tour of the grounds, serving us a lunch of stewed tomatoes and zucchini and rendering a melody by Brahms on her violin.

Shit! I'd been there! Same exact place.

Now was this synchronicity or what?

Wide eyed, I looked over at Mingus who was still droning on about the simple life. I was just about to leap into the conversation and tell him of our incredible parallel spiritual connection when, for no reason at all, he stopped talking, leaned back in his seat, and fell asleep. He was done with his mystical jive for the afternoon.

In five minutes, Mingus was snoring. One satisfied customer.

The plane landed about an hour into Charlie's nap. After collecting his precious briefcase and saying a few words to Danny, he deplaned. Apparently, he was in a big rush to connect with some lady in Mill Valley.

Along with the rest of the band, I went to a second-rate hotel in North Beach. I checked into my room then called my mother in L.A. She had promised me she would fly up to Frisco if circumstances permitted. Of course, what that really meant was if her *boyfriend* permitted. He was this rich dude who called all the shots and kept her on a short leash.

She must have negotiated some kind of deal with the guy, because fifteen minutes later she called back to tell me she'd be up in a couple of hours.

I was happy. Having Mom here would be a trip.

I glanced around the room. The joint was nothing to crow about. Dirty white walls, narrow twin beds, schlock art, yellowing lace curtains. The dresser and night-table were made of cheap particle board. Of course Mom would probably say it was quaint in order to spare my feelings.

I lay down to catch a few winks. A few minutes into Dreamland the phone rang.

"Hey, this is Danny. You all right?" I got it. Danny had assumed the role of my protector and care taker.

"Me and Clifford are going to Carmines for pizza later. I'll knock on your door, baby. O.K.?"

"Yeah man. Oh ... My mom will probably be in town by then. Can I bring her?"

"Sure baby. If she's your mom I know she's cool."

A few hours later Mom called up from the front desk. She walked in the room looking very nouveau. She was suited up in all black with hoop earrings and a little black lid on her head. She must have been reading the Bohemian handbook again. She *almost* looked hip, but of course she was still my mom.

"Hey man, what's shakin'?" I said to her as I opened the door.

At first she looked confused. She eyed me suspiciously.

"Are you on drugs?" Mom demanded.

"I'm high on life," I said trying to remember what some loopy flute player had once said to me. Of course, that statement was probably too profound for *her*.

She set her suitcase down on one of the beds and opened it.

"Here, Janie, I got you something."

It was a crocheted maroon top with tiny holes in strategic places. Maybe Mom was trying to turn me into some kind of artsy seductress. On second thought I kinda liked it, but I wasn't into looking femme. Hell, I wanted the cats to forget I was a chick.

"Thanks, man," I said as I hurriedly stuffed it in the bottom of my suitcase.

At dinner Danny won my mom over. Polite and intelligent, he actually seemed concerned about her well-being. Danny might have been a bad-boy at times, but he was quite functional in polite society. He had an amazing talent for smoothing things out. When mom complained about her soup being too cold, Danny silently motioned to the waiter and took care of the problem without a lot of hoopla. Voila! Steaming clam chowder — so hot you had to blow on it.

By eight thirty, we had all socialized and eaten. After some enthusiastic quibbling over who would pay the tab, Danny gallantly picked up the check.

It was almost gig time.

++++

The Jazz Workshop was a big barn-like place with rows of chairs in the front and middle of the room and tables in back. At the time, it was considered an important jazz venue.

I made sure Mom got a good seat, then I went over to the piano to try it out. A Steinway B. Far out. After running a few scales, I walked over to talk to Danny, who was setting up his drums. We were rapping when Mingus exploded through the door in a dramatic flurry. He walked over to the piano, plunked his charts down, and started tuning his bass, all in one grandiose motion. I started to say "Hey," then I decided perhaps it would be better to speak only when spoken to. The cat, as usual, was preoccupied.

Finally, he acknowledged me. "Do you remember that seven/four part in "Meditations?"

I nodded.

He grunted. You never really knew where you stood with this dude.

Mingus futzed with the mikes and tinkered with the knobs on the mixing board. Finally, we were ready to hit.

The first tune was easy. I thought I was handily holding my part down until I looked up and saw Mingus scowling, then setting his bass down. Clifford Jordan was burnin' and Danny Richmond was taking care of business, but Mingus had something on his mind. He was heading toward the piano, yelling something at me.

He leaned in close.

"Man, those aren't the right voicings. Think Duke Ellington. Ellington, baby." He stood in back of me shouting orders, then reached over my shoulders to demonstrate. I could feel the Big Dog's hot, alcohol-laced breath on my neck as he pounded out what he thought were the definitive chord voicings.

I glanced up at Danny. He averted my gaze.

A few bars later, Mingus walked back, picked up his bass and started playing again. I was all bent out of shape. I don't know if he meant to intimidate me but I kinda felt like the the Incredible Shrinking Man. But this was no movie.

The next few tunes he looked at me and yelled again. Mercifully he didn't bother to put down his bass. Shit, my *mom* was in the audience.

Then we came to "Meditations." It was one of those esoteric jazz suites with different movements, weird time signatures, and numerous key and tempo changes — a show dog's centerpiece.

When we came to the piano/bass solo, Mingus put his bass down again. This time, instead of just reaching over my shoulders, he forcibly nudged me off the piano bench with his hip. I felt really stupid as he demonstrated what I should have been playing. I just passively stood there, feeling dumb, arms dangling at my sides, wishing I was invisible.

On the break, I went over to talk to Mom, pretending nothing had happened. Yeah, like this kind of behavior was some normal occurrence on the bandstand.

We played one more set, Mingus gesticulating and yelling at me. Then, mercifully, the evening was over.

I was too depressed to even say goodnight to the guys. I collected Mom and we headed back to the hotel.

"You know Dollie," Mom said on the ride back, "why don't we go and listen to some Duke Ellington records tomorrow. Don't be so damn stubborn. You might get some ideas."

I held my tongue. Why couldn't I play the stuff like I *wanted* to play it? I had kind of a Bill Evans/McCoy Tyner spin on it. What was wrong with *that?*

I was in a complete state of angst as I turned off the light. The hard-assed bed wasn't helping either. I was longing for my old Salvation Army mattress. Did this kind of horrible stress and anxiety always accompany working a high-profile Big Dog gig?

Next morning Mom was buzzing around the room, full of good cheer. She had that stupid chirping sound in her voice that set my teeth on edge.

"I think we'll go out and find a cute little breakfast place..." she artfully paused, "then we'll stop by... I wonder if they have anything like Wallach's Music City up here?"

Mom had made up her mind that I was going to listen to the Duke today.

Soon we were in some big record store sampling a bunch of Duke Ellington L.P.'s. After digging the sounds for a few hours, I got the idea. Lots of flat fives and nines. Lots of dissonant melodic intervals. More like Monk than Bud. Groovy.

Mom and I spent the rest of the afternoon shopping. Her financier, the dude on the other end of the leash, had given her some extra bread for the trip, so she bought me a far out pair of high lace-up boots.

Over coffee I tried to paint a picture of the hip new life I was leading in the Big Apple.

I described my crib, explaining that the lack of furniture was simply due to my non-attachment to material things. As far as my friends, they all were hipper (and sometimes higher) than God. And as for the job opportunities — well check it out, wasn't I playing with one of the greats?

I was hoping I'd gotten through to her. We sat there a few minutes in the silence until Mom finally spoke.

"You *sure* you're not on drugs?"

++++

I played a lot of Ellington voicings that night. Mingus looked up and nodded a few times. I was also more familiar with the tunes, so I decided to take a few more liberties.

It was the middle of the second set. Mingus seemed like he was digging my playing more, when all of a sudden he put the bass down and stormed into the dressing room. It was directly in back of the bandstand, so even though the rest of the band was still playing, I could hear him crashing around in there.

Danny looked up and rolled his eyes. Clifford Jordan finished his solo as if nothing unusual had happened. I guess in Mingus' band the unusual was ordinary. When it came to my solo (which was sans bass), I faintly heard what I thought were tearing sounds coming from the dressing room.

What the hell was going *on?*

I tried to ignore the distraction coming from the dressing room, but it was hard to tune out all the thumping and ripping. What was the guy doing? Despite the distraction, I wound up my solo. Then Danny launched into a long drum cadenza. This was due to the fact that there was no bass, hence no bass solo.

Toward the end of the drum solo, Mingus emerged from the dressing room carrying what looked like long strips of terrycloth. Mingus had torn up a towel. For *what?*

He stepped up on the bandstand, heading for me — long terrycloth strips draped over his arm. For a fleeting second I thought he was going to tie me up.

I watched him in terror as he wordlessly made his move.

"What the...?" shit. Once again, Mingus pushed me off the piano bench, but this time it was for the purpose of getting under the piano. He wanted access to the pedals. Good God!! The Big Dog was fucking tying up my pedals! He was draping the terrycloth strips around all three pedals, tying them together so tightly that I wouldn't be able to depress them.

Finishing the job, he tested them a few times with his hands. Satisfied that the pedals were completely unusable, he strode back to his bass. Before picking it up he leveled his eyes at me.

"You use the pedal too much," Mingus seethed, mopping his brow with a spare piece of scavenged terrycloth. "It doesn't make you blow any better, man. *Chicks* use too damn much pedal anyway. I don't want to hear my stuff with all that fucking pedal!"

He said the word "chicks," with an inordinate amount of sibilance. I felt a twinge of hatred in the pit of my stomach.

Now I was *really* humiliated. Bummer. I tried to sit down on the piano bench, but my body wouldn't obey me. I turned toward the Big Dog. The next thing that came out of my mouth surprised even me.

"Fuck you man," I whispered, animatedly mouthing the words."You can't treat *me* that way."

Then I did something really weird. I got off the bandstand and went and sat in the audience, staring at him. Wow, I'd done some outside things before, but I had never tried to roll a Big Dog.

In my heart, I knew I was just a pup. But I guess I was so pumped up full of adrenalin, I was ready to scrap — even if my opponent was ten times bigger than me.

Mingus gave me an icy stare, and went back to playing his axe. He had a certain expertise at deflecting counter punches.

Since the incident happened on the second-to-last tune of the night, I continued to sit in the audience until the gig ended.

Mingus ignored me as he packed up, but Danny motioned me over as he covered his drums.

"Man, that cat's out," Danny said, shaking his head. "Listen, get your mom and we'll go out for some coffee. I got something I want you to check out."

Mom was all bent out of shape over my scrap with Mingus, so she decided to cab it back to the hotel. Danny and I wandered around until we found an all-night coffee shop in North Beach.

The night was nippy and I was shivering as we sat down. Danny took off his jacket and put around my shoulders.

"Listen, baby," Danny said, motioning to the waitress to bring us some menus. "I don't know if you're gonna dig this or not, but I know how you can change the vibe. I know this lady — a spiritualist. She's real good people and she can do some work on this situation. I've seen her completely turn things around. I mean like, boom! She's *heavy* man. I'd be happy to call her, darlin'. She'd love to see *you* Danny paused. "Wanna check it out?"

The guy was offering me *hope*. Hell, what could I lose? I mean I most definitely believed that there was some great cosmic force motivating things.

"I won't leave my room tomorrow 'til you call."

For the next few hours, I drank about five cups of coffee as Danny regaled me with tales about Mingus. Listening to the Mingus Chronicles gave me an entirely different perspective. Yeah, it wasn't me — the cat was just wigged out of his fucking skull.

++++

Danny called and gave me his friend's phone number. Her name was Rose. She lived in Sausalito.

I called and made an appointment with her.

I was all frazzled when I got there. Besides arguing with Mom about the advisability of seeing this lady, Rose's place was hell to find.

She lived on the very top of a hill in a small cottage, hidden in back of a big house. As I knocked on her door, I could hear wind chimes faintly in the background. In fact, everything seemed to be tinkling, like there were a hundred invisible, barely audible bells quietly chiming in my inner ear.

Her small garden, directly in front of her house, had flowers in the most vibrant pulsating shades of red and yellow I'd ever seen. And was I spacing out or were there rays of heat and light emanating from the perimeter of her house?

I blinked.

This was a magical place.

When she opened the door I knew that the vibe was right. This was no ordinary place and Rose was no ordinary woman.

Though she was physically tiny, her essence seemed to fill the entire space. And when she looked at you, you felt she was looking deep inside.

From the lines in her face I figured she was probably in her mid-sixties, but there was something about her that was neither young nor old. Danny was right — this lady was *authentic,* the real thing, baby.

Rose sat me down on her couch (an off-white overstuffed job) and went to fetch some herb tea. I looked around the room. It was filled with religious artifacts. I recognized a statue of the Goddess Kali, the six-armed destroyer, and a painting of the Virgin of Guadalupe. I liked that stuff. And the incense! It reminded me of all the delicious intriguing aromas I'd smelled as a child. It was like that wonderful perfume your mom was wearing when she gave you a big hug and held you safe in her arms.

I was trying to read some of the titles from her bookcase across the room when she came back with my tea.

"I hope you like clover-honey" Rose said, setting the steaming hot beverage down," "'cause that's all I've got today. I hear from Danny that you're a very talented young lady." She smiled, the lines in her face deepening. "He told me a little bit about your situation, but I need to ask you a few things."

I began at the beginning and ended at the point where I told Mingus to fuck himself.

"I wonder," I asked, "if you tell someone to fuck themselves does that mean you're automatically fired, or does it mean you're just pissed off?"

Rose smiled. "Jane, I think you're jumping to conclusions. You're not fired 'til you're fired. Know what I mean?"

I thought for a second. I did have a habit of picturing outcomes and filling in the blanks for other people.

"The first thing I'm going to have you do," Rose said, "is close your eyes. Then, I want you to visualize the person you're having problems with. When you have a good image of him in your mind, I want you to put a white light around him and see him as well, happy, peaceful, and calm. When you've accomplished "that, then visualize him as doing the right thing as far as your particular situation is concerned. Don't tell him what to do — just know he's going to do the right thing."

As she was speaking, I could see her going into a trance-like state herself, her eyes half-mast.

My first thought was, "How could this *possibly* work?" But I ignored it, closed my eyes, and proceeded to follow her instructions.

As I started to picture Mingus getting calm, I found myself cooling out as well. A wave of peace started to roll over me. I felt connected. The wind chimes seemed to be getting louder. But I wasn't sure if the sounds were external or internal.

I don't know how long Rose and I sat there, but when I opened my eyes, I felt a clarity about things. Rose smiled at me like she knew. The vibe was so cool I wanted to hang out all afternoon. But it was time to get get back to the hotel so I thanked her, gave her twenty-five beans, and split.

Back in my room, the message light on my phone was blinking.

"A Mr. Mingus called three times," the desk-clerk informed me, "But he didn't leave a number. He just said to meet him at the gig."

Ordinarily, I would have been freaked out, needing to know what he wanted, if I was still on the gig, what about this, what about that ... but today I put down the phone. *Whatever happens is going to happen when it happens.* I looked out the window and watched a few fluffy white clouds roll by and read.

++++

That afternoon, Mom checked out. The fat cat was tugging on her chain. Though I was in a good mood as I kissed her goodbye, I needed some time alone to revel in my new recently elevated state of mind.

I twirled around in the empty room a couple of times, then I decided to lie down for about an hour, *then* get dressed for the gig.

I was in such, a peaceful state I can't really say whether I fell asleep or not. All I know is I was feeling confident that whatever happened musically or otherwise would be in my best interest.

I floated through dinner, which was at another pizza joint, then cabbed it to the gig.

I arrived about fifteen minutes before we hit and spotted Mingus on the bandstand.

As I walked toward the bandstand, Mingus looked up, smiled, then motioned me over. Yessir, the Big Dog was beckoning me. He seemed to be glowing. The cat looked like some large, fluorescent, neo-bohemian Buddha. By the time I had reached the bandstand his smile had turned into a grin, wide as the Mississippi. He reached inside a shopping bag and handed me a smaller brown paper bag.

"These are for you," he said softly, like he was bestowing the *ultimate* gift on a faithful devotee.

Grasping the bag, I uncurled the top of the coarse brown paper.

Inside the sack were two boxes of strawberries, a bright red lipstick, and one pair of panty-hose, size small.

Huh?

Far out.

"Well thank you," I said.

"We're recording tonight," Mingus boomed, "and I want you on the record."

I went to the dressing room to hang up my coat and stash the Big Dog's peace offering. The vibe had indeed changed — Danny was right. But the most amazing thing about the whole episode, was that I wasn't trying to control anything anymore. Whatever the outcome was, would have been all right with me.

The rest of the night just rolled along. John Handy come in from Oakland to fill in some of the horn parts. He was burning.

Danny and Clifford were kickin' ass as usual and I was playing like I always played. But Mingus seemed to dig it. He still put his bass down and ran to the piano to play certain passages, but it didn't bother me. Mingus was being Mingus.

That night, I went back to my room, put on the red lipstick and ate the strawberries. As for the pantyhose, well that was another matter. Wearing pantyhose has always been a scary concept to me so I pretty much left them alone.

It's the thought that counts. Or so they say ....

++++

Mingus and I were on good terms when we returned to New York. I knew I'd probably work with him again in the future when his regular piano player, Jaki Byard couldn't make it. But in the meantime, I still had rent to pay.

I could see, just from the short time I was in the Big Apple, that the name of the game was hustling, calling people, making yourself known. The cats had short memories, so you'd damn well better show your face or give them a holler once in a while.

Time to get on the stick. Ring up some of the cats I knew. I went down my list; Pony Poindexter, George Braith, Carmel Jones, Thad Jones, Benny Maupin ...

2

THE SKIRT

I was drinking my late-morning coffee when I realized it had been a year since my gig with Mingus. I wasn't doing too badly. I still had my pad on ninety first street and was getting my fair share of gigs.

For a while now, I had been toying with the idea of buying some real furniture for my pad. I had just turned seventeen and purchasing some grown-up stuff would be like a rite of passage for me. People would think I *really* had my shit together.

I sat down on my salvation army cot/bed and checked out my crib. It was what was called a railroad-style apartment: a collection of rooms in a straight line, much like railroad cars. Those room were practically empty except for a salvation army bed, an upright piano, and a few boxes housing my earthly possessions. But hey, I was an artist. I wasn't suppose to have any domestic skills, was I?

Taking stock, I decided to start out modestly with a chest of drawers, then *eventually* work my way up to a couch. I was tired of rummaging through all my cardboard boxes every time I needed something. Besides, the cardboard itself was starting to shred and come apart.

I went to my cookie jar, got out fifty beans, then walked around the corner to check out of a little thrift shop on Amsterdam Ave. This was a good place to start. You couldn't go wrong with furniture someone else had already picked out and lived with.

Luckily, some old lady up the block had just died. Her son was hauling in a bunch of her stuff when I wandered in. I eyeballed the loot. Red velvet drapes, yellowed lace tablecloths, beautiful Wedgewood china. The works ... perfect! The dude had just carted in a groovy little chest of drawers. They looked like they had been around since the turn of the century. The wood had a warm reddish hue like rosewood and there were ornate wrough-iron handles hanging from the drawers.

There was only one slight problem. The bureau had a kind of acrid musty smell. It was probably an aromatic combo of moth balls, cedar wood, and time. I sniffed again. Yuk! It was the kind of smell that was in old people's houses. I'd always wondered where that smell came from. Was it that old folks smelled bad, or was it simply because their *furniture* was old?

Well, who cared. The thing looked good, so I decided to take it. The shop keeper assured me that the questionable odor would dissipate if I aired out the drawers by an open window and burned a little incense.

I thanked him, gave him twenty beans, and my address.

About an hour later, he delivered the thing. I immediately pulled out all the drawers and set the chest by an open window. Then I went to work sorting out the stuff in the cardboard boxes. I was just folding a few sweaters when the phone rang.

It was Pony Poindexter. Yep, I was still gigging with the alto player. Pony — my short little friend with eyes like small indigo marbles.

"Hey man, we got us a gig in Rochester next week."

Pony inhaled, taking a long drag on one of those humongous joints he liked to roll. "Better git ja a long coat, 'cause you're gonna freeze your little ass off up there if ya don't." Pony exhaled and coughed. "Hey baby, hold the phone. My old lady wants to talk to you."

There was a banging sound as Pony dropped the phone, then picked it up and handed it to his girlfriend, Louise.

"Hi Jane?" Today Pony's better half had a sweet little chirping sound to her voice. "Pony just told me about the gig and I've got a *great* idea." I pictured Louise sitting there next to Pony in all her midwestern uptightness. Yeah, Louise with her short straight bangs and straight white teeth .... But this conversation was starting to scare me. Anytime *that* girl had an idea .... Louise was sweet but she was the opposite of hip. She was from Minnesota.

"I've been talking to Pony about the band image," Louise said casually, "and I think it would be super if you wore a skirt. A *long* skirt would look *so* classy on you."

The word "skirt" acted like a trigger mechanism. I could feel my anxiety level rising. I mean, what if I had to run a hundred-yard dash, or jump over a few tables? Or suppose the place caught on fire? Or — what if I had to punch someone out?

"Louise, I don't know about that, " I said. "I mean, what if I had a situation that required, you know, a lot of mobility?"

"I've already figured that out," she said knowingly. "We'll make the skirt full enough to accommodate any situation."

We bantered back and forth. Finally I gave in. There was simply no arguing with Louise.

++++

About five days later I met up with Pony, Louise, (drummer) Marvin Patillo and (bassist) Don Baily at Port Authority.

The old wood-paneled station wagon we usually tooled around in, was having problems. I was secretly glad. Besides the upholstery being ripped and the springs poking you in the butt, (which I hated), the engine needed a major overhaul.

Pony decided not to chance it. We were taking the bus. I overheard him grumbling about having to shell out the bread for our fares, but he was a known complainer so no one paid much attention.

After listening to a few more seconds of Pony's griping, we split off into a few little groups: Marvin and I into one unit, Pony and Louise into another. Don, who was known as a spacecase and apparently communed with beings who were elsewhere, formed his own unit.

We stood around in our own separate worlds until Louise walked up to me and handed me a brown paper bag.

"Here's the skirt, baby," she said nonchalantly. "It's black, so I'm sure that any top will go perfectly with it."

I was hoping she'd forgotten about the damn thing but there it was. Wearing *that* thing would be like making a formal announcement that I was . a chick. That was the *last* fucking thing I wanted.

"Thanks man," I said a bit dejectedly. I started to set the garment down with the rest of my luggage; then on impulse, I peeked in the bag. It was worse then I'd imagined. The monstrosity had an elastic waistband — guaranteed to make even a skinny bean-pole chick look fat. It was plug-ugly, not to mention home-made — the fashion kiss of death.

For diplomacy's sake I'd have to wear the stupid thing at least once — until it conveniently ripped or was somehow damaged.

++++

A light snow was just beginning to fall as we boarded the bus. I sat next to my pal Marvin, executing a few subtle maneuvers so I could sit to the right of him. That way, I wouldn't have to look at the deformed side of his head. Marvin was actually a groovy looking dude, but unfortunately nature had forgotten to give him a left ear. The doctors had tried to fashion a new one for him, but being it was the mid sixties, plastic surgery was still in its infancy. The faux ear looked like someone had stuck a dark-brown seashell somewhere on the left side of his head. But Marvin was surprisingly unself-conscious about his deformity. He didn't make others feel guilty about *his* problem. Now *that* was an alright guy.

I hadn't seen Marvin in a while, so we had a lot of catching up to do. Maybe taking the bus wasn't such a bad idea. The little white flakes drifting by the window had a calming effect. For a moment I forgot about the fashion monstrosity in the bag, Marvins ear, and the freezing weather right outside the window.

The Greyhound had been rollin' down the highway at a nice clip and I was busy rappin' about Carmel Jones — this great trumpet player I had worked with at Birdland — when the bus jerked, skidded, and then came to a sudden stop. The light snowfall had, in the blink of an eye, become a blizzard. As I looked out the window, the sky was now spewing forth a furious white flurry.

As there was zero visibility, the driver decided to do the prudent thing: stop.

Pony didn't agree with his decision. He flipped out, like I'd seen him do numerous times before. The cat started to snarl as the veins on his forehead popped out. Fact is, every second we remained immobile, Pony got even more uptight, stamping his feet and yelling abusive things to the driver. Finally, he strode up to the front of the bus and *really* started in on the cat. For a second I thought the two of them were going to get into it.

"Shit man, every minute we're stuck here I'm losing money," Pony hissed. "If we miss the first night, I have to *pay* the cats anyway. I'm outta pocket. *Do you understand, mother fucker?"*

For a second there was complete silence.

"I apologize, sir," the bus driver said cautiously, "but there are certain safety precautions we *must* follow. I'm sorry you're losing money but I can't jeopardize the lives of my passengers." The guy sounded like driving a bus was some kind of a mission from on-high. This could have been a scene from *"The High and the Mighty"* where pilot, John Wayne, in order to save the passengers, threw the baggage out of the plane. Hey, maybe the bus driver would heroically throw the bag with my double ugly black skirt out!

But things were going from bad to worse. Pony had broken into a sweat. His steely black eyes were fixed on poor Mr. Busdriver. Oh yeah, that lowly peasant was refusing to obey one of King Pony's royal edicts. But though Pony tightened the noose, no amount of cajoling, begging, demanding, or even threatening to kill the driver's immediate family could make the driver fire up the engine. So there we were — stuck in the middle of nowhere until the foul weather abated.

Hours later, we sputtered into the next Greyhound Terminal, a small claustrophobic little hole in the wall. Pony — all bent out of shape — called the clubowner to tell him about the weather conditions and prepare him for our late arrival.

The club owner wasn't buying Pony's line. As I walked down the hall to the restroom, I could hear Pony trying to convince the guy that we weren't responsible for Mother Nature's little rampage.

"No, indeed," Pony said tersely. "A blizzard is what I would call an Act of God, and every contract *I've* ever seen has an Act of God clause in it. Check it out. We didn't *intend* to be late. How the hell ...."

Pony's voice trailed off as I spotted the facilities. I quickly let myself into a big door with a "W" on it and flipped the latch. I not only had to relieve myself, I had to get away from Pony's tiresome rap. I needed the luxury of some peace and quiet.

Revived and relieved, I opened the restroom door. As I stepped into the hall, two guys with crewcuts were standing there, blocking my way. One was tall and one was short and squat. Not exactly a legal midget (4'7"), but pretty low to the ground. Where the hell did they come from? The pair looked like Mutt and Jeff.

"That looks like her," the tall guy said.

As I looked up at him, I noticed his face was pockmarked and he had a bulbous nose, the tip of it being red and shiny. Very Rudolphian.

I tried to smile and make a quick exit to the waiting room when the short stubby guy grabbed my arm.

"Hey baby, are you Julia Sarentino?"

"Who the hell's that?" I said trying to keep my composure.

"A runaway. She's about twelve, your height weight, and coloring. Do you have any I.D.?" the tall crewcut said.

Now I know I had a young face, but I thought I looked pretty sophisticated in my high black lace up boots and tight midriff-baring jeans. How could they think *I* was twelve?

I started to reach into my purse for my I.D. when Pony walked through the door.

He looked at Mutt and Jeff. They looked at him. Each one thinking the worst.

"Take your hands off that girl!" Pony shouted. "She's in my band."

"What band is that?"

Uh oh. The midget had challenged Pony.

"My jazz band, you fucking retard."

They thought that Pony was harboring a runaway and had some kind of shady operation going. Maybe I was a young filly in Pony's stable. They weren't about to give me up until Pony gave them some proof he was a legit musician.

Pony sprinted out to the lobby, opened his sax case and took out his axe. He then started into a chorus of Charlie Parker's "Scrapple from the Apple." By the time he walked into the hallway, he was burnin.' Maybe the fuzz thought that Pony knew too many Bird licks to be a badass street-hustler. Whatever their rationale, they reluctantly let me go by the time Pony had reached his last eight bars.

The two walked away shaking their heads, not sure of just what had gone down.

Unfortunately, this incident confirmed Pony's suspicions that circumstances were conspiring against him.

++++

The cab screeched to a halt in front of this funky old club — Rochester's finest and only jazz joint. Our gig that night was theoretically half over when we arrived.

Marvin quickly unloaded his drums and set up. Don unzipped his bass case, pulled out his axe, and tuned up. I ran to the ladies room opened my suitcase and put on a tight black sweater. As an afterthought I put on the skirt Pony's old lady had whipped up. Maybe seeing his lady's handiwork would elevate Pony's mood.

I hurriedly applied some fresh makeup and ran up to the bandstand. Pony had just starting counting off the first tune: "Basin Street." The cat was humming, bouncing his head, and snapping his fingers like he usually did, when all of a sudden he aborted the count off.

"What's that smell?" Pony angrily whispered.

Pony scrunched up his nose, then zeroed in on my sweater which had been housed in the old chest of drawers I had just purchased. I smelled like a combination of mothballs, incense, and Granny's house.

Shooting me a dirty look, Pony walked to the other side of the stage to reboot the tune.

He didn't speak to me for the rest of the evening.

At the end of the night, Pony and Louise left wordlessly. They crashed at the clubowner's house while the rest of the band ambled upstairs to the musicians quarters. This was one long-assed tiring day.

Our accommodations consisted of three tiny rooms, each of which had peeling linoleum floors, torn window-shades, and prison-type cots with balled-up, dirty cream-colored blankets. The place had a faint cat-urine smell, but as far as I could see, there were no cats. Par for the course.

There was also no heat in the joint. It was too cold to take off your clothes so I decided to sleep in my skirt, sweater, and long coat. I'd seen a guy in a magazine with frostbite once and it wasn't a pretty picture.

When I awoke the next morning the windows were steamed up and my clothes were wrinkled and covered with lint. I was also sweating because the heat had gone on sometime during the night. I was sure I looked and smelled like something the nonexistent cat had dragged in. Now the skirt Pony's old lady had made looked like a misshapen, wrinkled rag with an elastic band around it. Great. The day was not off to a good start.

++++

The next night the weather had cleared up a bit. As I walked downstairs from the band's quarters, I could see that the club was packed. I smiled at Pony as I got on the the bandstand. I had taken great pains to slick my hair back in a neat little pony tail so he wouldn't notice how wrinkled and linty my clothes looked.

The ploy didn't work. Pony eyeballed me for a second, than turned away. Tonight I looked *and* smelled bad.

Pony, who was usually very forthcoming and gregarious was acting very subdued and businesslike. I knew something was up. But what? I was getting paranoid. Maybe the cat had called Cedar Walton or John Hicks to replace me. I started to visualize being fired and going home alone on the bus. Shit, all the cats in New York would be talking about the little jive gig I'd messed up.

My playing was off. My thoughts were elsewhere. I felt frustrated and helpless. What the hell was bugging Pony? I needed to take some action, but on what front? What could *I* do?

Then it came to me.

Deep-six the skirt.

As Pony ended the last tune of the first set, I spotted a loud drunk red-haired lady carelessly waving a cigarette. She had that Dodge City look about her. She would do. I strolled up and stood beside her, waiting for her to make some stupid uncoordinated gesture, I'd seen lots of wasted chicks make. Yes indeed, maybe Miss Kitty would burn a neat little hole in that butt-ugly piece of polyester.

The cat next to her made some lame joke. She proceeded to laugh while at the same time raising her arms and flailing her hands in the air. As she did that, the glowing spark at the end of her cigarette met the side of my skirt. But instead of burning a hole in my skirt as planned, the stray ember rolled off the garment and unto my foot. I felt a stab of pain as the live red-hot end of her cigarette burned a hole in my black tights and seared the skin on my foot.

Shit! I knew I should have worn my high lace-up boots. Why the hell did I have to be so vain with all that ballet slipper crap? After all I wasn't the chick from *Swan Lake*.

Now I was limping around with torn black tights and a lint covered wrinkled up skirt, smelling like a Granny Zoo. I gimped up to the bandstand for the second set. Pony looked down and eyeballed my torn tights. He shook his head. For the past few days the cat had been preoccupied with something. It felt like Pony was gathering evidence against me. *Why?* At the end of the second set Marvin motioned me over.

"What's with Pony?" Marvin whispered. Even level-headed, even-tempered Marvin was puzzled.

"Damned if *I* know. But I do know one thing, man — that truth is stranger than fiction."

Marvin laughed, then eyeballed my sweltering red sore. "What happened to your foot, man?"

"Oh just a minor accident," I said casually, trying to dismiss the pain. "Ain't nothin'."

"Better put something on it, before it gets infected," Marvin said, peering at my wound which already beginning to fester.

Marvin had momentarily forgotten about Pony as he eyeballed my appendage, but Pony hadn't forgotten about *us*. He had surreptitiously wound around the back of the room and was silently standing next to us. When I looked up my eyes met his.

"I want to see both you cats after the third set. We'll meet in the kitchen," Pony said menacingly.

During the next set, I tried my best to concentrate. When Pony played "Confirmation," I took a great solo. I was immersed in the music, connecting all the dots and tying up all the loose ends. Then the set was over. Reality set in.

Pony jumped off the bandstand and motioned us into the kitchen. The three of us unhappily plodded into the greasy smelling furnace. Ed, the cook, was just lowering his last batch of fries into the bubbling oil when we walked in.

"We're closin' the kitchen guys." Ed informed us.

Mr. Ed (as the band called him) was tattooed, and pockmarked. He'd been a cook aboard one of the vessels in the Merchant Marines. *I* could tell he was experienced by the deft way he moved his wrist when he flipped the burgers over.

"We don't want nothin' now," Pony said. "I got some band business to discuss."

Pony led us to a little spot in back, near the freezer.

Then he lowered his head and looked up at us with his hard black eyes. "I got some bad news for you. Remember the argument I had with the clubowner when I was on the phone in the bus station? Well the cat decided, since we weren't here at the agreed time, he was gonna dock us. Sorry but I'm gonna have to take some of it out of your bread."

Then Pony levelled his headlights at me. "I'm docking *you* even more — 'cause of your behavior this week. Yeah girl, you've been giving me too much shit. I just *don't* appreciate it. Hell no. Uh uh."

My *behavior?* What the hell was he talking about? I'd been alternately freezing my ass off and burning up in that flophouse upstairs, wearing a lame-assed skirt just because his old lady had made it, in addition to trying to cope with the crap *he* was dishing out.

I stared at him, my mouth curling into a wordless frown.

"I'm cuttin' *your* bread down a hundred bucks!"

Now the cat had overstepped his boundaries. Cuttin' my bread down? One hundred beans?

My hand curled into a fist. All the free rehearsals I had made with this cat. All the times he had post-dated my checks so he could buy some weed. All the funky flea bag motels we stayed in so that little sucker could save some bread. All that shit flashed through my mind. Then I remembered the time when I had a stuffed nose and Pony handed me this inhaler and told me it was Vicks. *Like hell it was!* When I sniffed that thing I felt like I was going to die. The fucker had given me a popper and almost killed me!

I swung my balled-up fist at his nose.

Luckily, Marvin caught it in mid-air.

Pony stood there absolutely frozen in disbelief.

"Whoa! Whoa man! " Pony yelled as Marvin held my trembling fist in the air. "Who was the first cat to give ya a gig in New York? And don't think I didn't get a *lot* of crap from the *brothers* about hiring you."

Little rivulets of sweat had started to form on Pony's forehead. "Shit, being on the road would be *much* easier if I didn't have some *chick* who had to go to the John every five minutes or always had to have her own little motel room or insisted on ratting up her damn fucking hair while the cats waited in the lobby. Hey baby, it's me not *you* thats goin' the extra mile. All those little extras are comin' out of my pocket. *I'm* takin' the hit. All I'm askin' you to do is work with me a little. I've got your best interest at heart."

When did *that cat* become my father? I could almost see him clutching his chest and telling me that I was giving him a heart attack.

Slowly, I lowered my arm and mulled over what he had just said. *I* thought he had hired me because I took care of business. Now he was intimating I was some kind of charity case — some poor little despised white chick.

I looked over at Mr. Ed. He was scraping the grill. Now *there* was a cat with integrity. He just did his job and went home. Why couldn't *I* do that? Why did playing in a band have to be such a fiasco?

By now, Marvin had loosened the grip on my fist. But now I had inched my way close enough to Pony to make a lightning move and reshape the little fucker's nose. I was sick of Pony's bullshit.

I felt a surge of adrenalin.

Deliberately, I brought my fist up again. Before Pony knew it my fist was again flying toward Pony's septum. My hand stopped a hair's breath short of making a connection.

I stood there for a second with my frozen fist almost touching the tip of Pony's nose, my lip curled above my teeth in a wolf-like sneer and my eyes narrowed. Now *I* was the menacing one, the stalker, the imminent threat.

It felt good. Almost *too* good.

Checkmate Pony.

We just stood there eyeing each other for a moment. Then a sheepish grin appeared on Pony's face. He cracked a smile.

"You're okay baby," Pony said. "I always knew you had balls. Just do me one favor. *Lose* the skirt!! I never want to see that damn thing on you again!"

After the gig, I put the odious piece of polyester in the incinerator downstairs. Then I lit a match.

++++

Pony still docked my bread for that gig. But he had a newfound respect for me. He deferred to me a lot now. I got to put my two cents in as to where the band stayed and who he hired as subs. Most importantly, I had proven one thing to myself. You *could* actually punch someone in the nose while wearing a skirt. But that didn't mean I was ever going to wear one again.

On second thought, who was Pony to tell me I didn't look good in a skirt. Shit, maybe I'd get a short little micro mini. I liked that Mary Quant look.

As for the chest of drawers, I aired them out again when I got home, but just like cat urine, the smell lingered on. I finally ended up calling the Salvation Army to haul the thing away. In return, they agreed to give me a sizeable discount on another dresser or the couch of my choice.

Yeah man, now I was wheelin' and dealin'.

3

HERBIE THE MANN

Pony Poindexter was in New Orleans attending someone's
funeral. He said he'd probably be back in a couple of weeks,
but you never knew with Pony. A couple of weeks could turn
into a couple of months — what with all his skirt-chasing and
imbibing of that weird green aromatic plant he liked to smoke.

Though Pony had been my main source of gigs for a
while now I couldn't depend on his largesse in the near future.
It was time to call some other cats in town, check out some
different prospects.

I needed some bread — and bad — because I had
spent most of my savings (less than a hundred bucks) on a
used dresser and couch. Though the dresser was fairly cheap,

the Salvation Army couch was a little pricey because, as the saleslady explained, it was *almost* new.

It was also kind of space-age or, more accurately, what someone in the 1930's would have considered "modern." Added on to that, it was *huge,* measuring nearly seven feet in length with gull-wing armrests and a back which curved outward like a turned up collar. I couldn't pinpoint what style it was, but it didn't matter. My new acquisition would serve the purpose of furthering my musical agenda.

Now I could invite some of the cats over, like Carmel Jones, George Braith, or Joe Chambers, a young drummer who I had a secret crush on. These were some of the new happening cats in town that were starting a buzz. I wanted to connect. After *those* guys saw my new furniture, they would stop thinking of me as just some unsophisticated naive kid.

I *was* making all my own money and supporting myself, wasn't I?

And now I not only had a new chest of drawers in the bedroom, *I* had a couch to boot. How much more adult could you get than *that?*

I gazed fondly at my new purchase, then went and plopped down on it.

I also brought a pad of paper and a pencil with me so I could compile a list of piano players who might throw a few gigs my way.

I'd just written Horace Parian's name down when I had a flash.

I ran over to my phone book and looked up Chick Corea's number. Now *that* cat had gigs coming out of his ears. He also had called me a few times when I'd been busy, so I knew he considered me good "sub" material.

I dialed Chick's number. *Ring, ring ring.* Shit, c'mon.

I was ready to hang up when someone picked up the line.

"Hello?" Chick was out of breath.

"Hi Chick? Hey man, this is Jane Getz. So ah, what's happening?"

"Jane! Oh man, I just walked in the door. Can I call you back in five? I've got some macrobiotic takeout I gotta put in the fridge."

"Sure." I hung up the phone and plunked down on my new couch to wait.

Uh, oh. Did I feel a lump? I started to run my hands over the tightly woven, scratchy upholstery when the phone rang.

"Yeah?"

"Hey baby, Chick here. Listen, are you still working with Pony?"

"Man, the cat's out of town. He kinda checked out on me for a minute. Whats shakin'?" I was trying to sound confident while at the same time conveying a feeling that I was musically up for anything.

"I'm thinkin' of going on the road with Joe Henderson, but I have to get a sub for this gig with Herbie Mann. Fact, I'm working with Herbie today over at the Apollo. It would be cool if you could come by, play a few numbers with the cat and let him hear you. The bread's not bad either."

"Thanks man, just give me the address and time. I'm already there."

++++

A few hours later I arrived at the Apollo Theater. A big old boxy building comprised of huge slabs of old sandy-colored stone. Following Chick's directive, I went around back and walked up some clangy steel steps. The guard, a strapping young dude with that Malcolm X bowtie getup, stood by the backstage entrance. The brother asked me my name, looked me up and down a few times, then checked my name off a rather short list.

I walked in and adjusted my eyes to the dim half light. Wow! The place was jam packed. The audience was having a grand old time screaming and laughing at some rotund funny-man who was strutting around the stage, talking about all the edible parts of a pig. I stood there digging the scene for a minute, then went to search for Chick.

I nosed around backstage till I finally spotted him sitting in the wings near the food table, reading a book on Macrobiotics. He was checking out the No. 7 diet — a very strict regimen. Damn. Chick was wafer thin now. After a few bars of conversation, I followed him to a small dressing room to see Herbie Mann.

Herbie was sorting out some music as we entered the room. He didn't even bother to look up.

I knew the game. I'd seen other Big Dogs do this.

I stood there trying to be unobtrusive while at the same time, checking the dude out.

I could see by the way Herbie handled the music, that every move he made was deliberate. He was a planner. A guy with a road map who had memorized the route. Even the space around him was organized. The dressing room chairs were all perfectly lined up, the bottled water had cups neatly stacked next to it, and his toiletry kit was open and ready — every clipper, tweezer, and nail file in it's proper slot.

Oh yeah — *this* cat was all business. Much too neat for *my* taste with his closely-cropped, thinning brown hair, neatly trimmed goatee, and manicured nails. Nothing happenstance or spontaneous about *him*. He looked like some Upper East-Side decorator had turned him out. His freshly-ironed navy blue shirt was perfectly coordinated with his beige slacks. Casual tan suede shoes matched the soft leather belt he had on. Mr. Mann was one stiff dude.

After Herbie finished what he was doing, he finally looked up and greeted us.

"Jane Getz," Herbie said nonchalantly. "I've been hearing a lot of good things about you. I hope you'll play a few tunes with us."

"Thanks man, I'd like to," I said, trying to get that team player sound in my voice. "I hear the band is smokin'. Yeah, you got some *bad* cats." I was talking about Dave Pike, the young vibes player, Bruno Carr, the drummer and Potato Valdez, the little badass from Cuba who played conga's.

The three of us stood there rapping for a few minutes until Herbie excused himself, scurrying out of the room to round up the rest of the band. After we exited, Chick and I walked around to the stage entrance and waited while the Master of Ceremonies made some lame jokes about fat chicks. About ten minutes later he finally got around to announcing the band.

"Ladies and Gentlemen ... put your hands together and give a grand Apollo welcome to the inimitable Herbie Mann and his..."

Herbie sprinted on stage with the band in tow and immediately gave the down beat. Dave Pike played a little vibe cadenza then Herbie motioned to Potato. The little cat hit the conga a few times. The rhythm started to engulf us. You could see the streets of Cuba alive with chattering, animated Cubanos: gentlemen in white suits and panama hats regally strolling down the lane puffing on cigars, and high spirited *senoritas* parading around in their pastel finery, strutting their stuff. The sounds were chili-pepper hot. By the time Herbie came in with his flute, the mood was established.

Oh yeah, and I also noticed that Chick had a hip way of playing the *claves*. I made a mental note to have Chick show me some of that *real* legit Latin stuff.

Impressed though I was with Herbie's onstage entourage I was apprehensive as I stood in the wings. I not only wanted Herbie to think I was *bad*, I also wanted to impress Chick.

By the time the maestro introduced me, my anxiety had given me a slight edge. I was on top of it now.

I sat down at the piano. The audience, already fired up by the first couple of tunes, was about as enthusiastic as any audience could get. At the mere mention of my name (someone they had never even heard of), they started stamping their feet, clapping, and whistling. Cool. This was a win-win situation. Predictably, after I took my first solo on a tune called "Walkin'," they went bonkers.

Herbie started nodding his head when he saw the audience's reaction. Alright!! I had just become another added attraction in the cat's musical sideshow.

"Yeah baby, that was some nice work," Herbie said as we walked back to the dressing room. "If you wanna do the gig at the Gate tomorrow, you got it!! In fact, if you're up for it, just meet me in front of my building at 7:00 tomorrow. I can show you the book while we're riding downtown."

"Cool man," I said trying to sound casual. "Ah, where do you live?"

++++

As I walked out of the theater I looked at the slip of paper with Herbie's address on it. I knew *approximately* where it was. I decided to catch a cab back from the Apollo so I would pinpoint the exact street and building.

As I suspected, Herbie lived a scant block from me, but that block — being this was New York City — was an entire universe away. The cat lived in the lap of luxury. I knew his building. It was a swank impenetrable fortress with a 24-hour-a-day doorman, a message service at the front desk, and a huge sweeping sloping ambient green roof garden. Herbie lived *on* Central Park West and Ninety First Street — where the rich *and* getting richer were domiciled. I simply lived on Ninety First Street *between* Central Park West and Amsterdam, where the working stiffs, scrapers, and starving artists hung.

Motoring by, I wondered if I'd ever live in such sumptuous surroundings or have anything to show for my mystical moments of creativity. What did it really take to get there?

But it was just a fleeting thought. Fuck it. Who needed a jungle on their roof anyway? *I* had more important things to do.

I was going to study my Slonimsky book later and see if I could lift a few hot licks from it. This was a book with strange repetitive intervals and offbeat sound patterns. A book Shoenberg might have glanced at. I'd even heard that Coltrane found a *lot* of shit in *that* book. Tonight I was going to pour over the pages and see if I could uncover some of the musical secrets some of the Big Dogs seemed to have accessed.

++++

The next day I prepared for the gig by practicing a little, and lounging on my couch. The damn thing seemed to have petrified — it was as hard as a rock, with a few little marble sized bumps to make you even more uncomfortable. Oh well....

As the sun went down, I got dressed then visited the bodega around the corner where I got a quick sandwich. After scarfing down a few dry slices of turkey on stale wheat bread, I sprinted down the block to Herbie's crib.

As I got there I saw the doorman was holding the door. Herbie waved to me, then proceeded to introduce me to a woman — presumably his wife — who had exited the building with him.

"Jane, this is my wife Ruth. Ruth — meet Jane Getz, my new pi-a-nist.

Ruth smiled listlessly, making a feeble attempt to nod. She was fashionably turned out, the same ultra-straight way a secretary might be. Her knee-length royal blue mohair suit was expensive, but boring. Her auburn hair was smartly cut. But she was wearing so much Spray Net her hair looked like a helmet. And why was she wearing those button earrings? The chick had no fashion sense. Nada. Zip.

I glanced at Ruth's shoes. I was just about to critique her footwear when some cat who looked like an officer in Napoleon's Army ran into the street and hailed a cab. Why did doormen need military uniforms?

I hastily climbed in, then watched as Herbie and Ruth maneuvered their way in. They positioned themselves so as not to touch or brush up against one another. The signs were clear. They didn't like each other.

I instantly came to the conclusion that there was some kind of weird "arrangement" between them. I didn't know the specifics — but I knew it was there.

Traveling downtown with Herbie and Ruth was creepy. It was more than just uncomfortable with all the bad vibes they were generating. And where were all the charts Herbie was going to show me?

I sat there rigidly, looking straight ahead until the vehicle came to a halt. I breathed a sigh of relief as I saw the sign that said Village Gate.

Then I saw the marquee.

Wow! Miles Davis was headlining. One of my heroes. A Big Dog Supreme. For a moment I couldn't catch my breath. To think! I was in a band playing opposite the great Miles!

Now I was pumped up. I floated out out onto the curb in front of this huge stone edifice while Herbie and Ruth wordlessly separated.

I walked a little behind Herbie into the lobby. We were silently milling about until two girls, who looked to be in their mid-teens walked up to the maestro and linked arms with him. Herbie smiled. He was expecting them. At *that* point I became extraneous. Just so much baggage until he needed me.

I strolled to the other side of the room and found a big double door on the far end of the lobby that opened into the main room, a big barn-like drafty space, with hundreds of little tables all scrunched together. A few customers who had arrived early were sitting around drinking and regaling their fellow jazz lovers with little-known anecdotes about about some of the jazz greats.

"Hey didja hear what Miles said to Cannonball when he ...."

I scurried past the enclave of noisy tables, smiled at a waiter who happened to be walking by, then found another door and wandered down a long dimly lit hallway. Suddenly, I heard what sounded like loud laughter and hornplayers warming up.

I entered the band room and stood there for a second. Potato Valdez walked over and greeted me, graciously extending his hand. He had calloused green little fingers with swollen knuckles. The tiny Cuban (he was about 5'2") gripped my hand, ceremoniously pumping my arm like some Third

World game show host. After giving me what he considered a sufficient welcome, Potato turned to Dave Pike and grinning broadly, said, "she an eenious."

Naturally, being called an "eenious" by the esteemed Potato gave me a jolt of self confidence not to mention credibility with the the band. I was on a roll, chatting and joking around with the cats. I felt a certain amount of camaraderie with the band as we all exited the dressing room and walked down the dark corridor toward the stage. The vibe was cool.

The first set was pretty smooth. So far, the only thing that was bugging me was that everyone in the band except Herbie was relegated to taking two or three-chorus solos.

You couldn't stretch out, get a fire going or come to any kind of musical climax when you were allotted *that* amount of solo time. Hell no!

Personally, *I* liked to take at *least* fifteen choruses. So what if I bored everyone silly? I was an artist and entitled to take liberties. Still ... this was my first night on the gig. Too soon to make waves or even do a little body surfing.

During the first break I grabbed a seat in the audience so I could listen to the headliner. Oh yeah, I wasn't going to miss a note of Miles' band.

Listening to Herbie Hancock, Wayne Shorter, Ron Carter, Tony Williams, and Miles sent me into the stratosphere. Herbie was playing unique little counter rhythms to Tony's innovations. The rhythm section sounded like a Fourth of

July fireworks show with little constantly exploding surprises. Miles weaved in and out of the mix, like a Martian tap-dancer strutting on some lunar bayou. You had no idea where he was coming from, but still, it was familiar like an old folk melody that was just out of earshot.

The band was burnin'. I noticed that when someone in *that* aggregation took a solo, they could play as long as they damn pleased.

I was both euphoric and jealous.

The next set with Herbie was even more frustrating. How could anyone who could improvise well take just two or three choruses? There were so many great players in the band but nobody was getting to play.

I needed some space.

++++

During the next break I decided to go outside the club to get some air. The West Village had some cute little shops that were open far into the night, so I thought I'd stroll down the street and do some window shopping.

Walking down the steps of the Gate, a low, raspy unmistakable voice said, "Hi Jane."

Was it?

No way.

It couldn't be.

But as he stepped out of the shadows of the old stone building, I saw his face.

Miles Davis, the Musical Maestro Supreme had acknowledged me. The Great Trumpet god had ....

I felt a knot in the pit of my stomach.

A million thoughts flipped through my mind. I wondered if he'd been listening to me during the last set? How did he know my name? And should I say "Hi Miles," or "Hello Mr. Davis," or should I simply turn around and try to strike up a conversation?

Not knowing what to do I stiffly nodded my head, and looking straight ahead, kept right on walking.

As I continued down the block I started to feel weak, like I was going to throw up. I could have kicked myself. What kind of idiot keeps right on walking when *Miles Davis* says hello?

Oh man, I had blown it.

I walked back on the bandstand a half an hour later depressed as hell.

To make matters worse, Herbie repeated some dopey show tune from the *The Smell of the Grease Paint, Roar Of The crowd*. A tune where he furiously gyrated his hips while spurting out an endless barrage of high notes.

I abstractedly took my requisite two choruses. I really wasn't into it. All I could think of was "Miles" had said hello to me.

Being on this gig was like being a musical civil servant. *Punch the clock.* Collect your bread. This was the low end of the Jazz food-chain.

Next tune was a minor blues by Oliver Nelson. I yawned, looked at my watch, then glanced around the room in a one-eighty.

Oh God!

I couldn't believe it.

Yep — there he was. Miles was sitting right behind me. No doubt about it. *He was checking me out.* Knowing I'd spotted him, he looked up and almost imperceptibly nodded.

It felt like there was some kind of radiant heat coming from his direction. My back actually started to feel hot.

Miles was emanating!

Now it was a whole new ballgame.

When Herbie counted off the next tune I was already in high gear, hyper alert and conscious of every lick, chord, and rhythmic pattern I was playing.

Now Herbie was out of the picture. I was only concerned about what the guy who was burning a hole in my back was thinking.

The tune was slow getting under way, but by the time Dave Pike took his solo, there was a nice groove happening. After Dave's mandatory two choruses, Herbie pointed to the trombone player, Mark Weinstein. Mark stood up and sailed along on the groove until *his* time was up. Then Herbie looked at me and nodded.

O.K. pal. *My* turn.

By the time I had gotten midway through the second chorus, I was on fire. My fingers were literally flying over the keys. But unfortunately, it was time for the band to come in.

Herbie raised his arms in a big flourish, giving the signal for the band to enter.

No, wait ....

I wasn't finished yet.

I vehemently shook my head, signaling the aggregation not to come in.

They followed my lead.

I could see Herbie out of the corner of my eye getting uptight. His loyal subjects had defied him. He was looking like "what the *fuck?*"

When my next chorus was over Herbie *again* tried to bring the band in. Sorry. I had *more* to say. Now I was doing a very difficult run in the upper register. Something I hadn't been able to execute before.

The great Trumpet god was giving me power.

The heat penetrating my back started to percolate through my whole body like a hot oil message.

Was this osmosis?

For the second time, I gave a "no go" sign to the band.

Herbie's face had become scarlet red. The poor guy looked like he had gotten too much sun on his roof garden.

For a minute I felt completely weightless. My fingers were faster then the speed of light.

I took two more choruses, then stood up and ceremoniously waved the band in.

I looked over at Herbie. His face was frozen. The only thing moving was his jaw which was traveling up and down in a kind of mandibular Hokey Pokey.

On the brighter side, the rest of the cats were beaming. Potato, surreptitiously stuck his little green thumb up. I had a cheering section.

Unfortunately, Herbie was *not* in that aggregation.

When the set was over, he asked me to meet him in the lobby.

My stomach started to knot up. I had slew of emotions. Sure, I had just bucked the system, challenged the status quo and all that crap. But now what?

I glanced around to check out the table in back of me.

Shit!

It was empty.

Miles had split.

++++

I thought about what had transpired. I did something every cat in the band had *wanted* to do but didn't have the guts to. On the other hand I had also *screwed myself.* Yeah, after Herbie *fired* my ass, who did I think was going to pay my rent, phone bill, gas, electric, etc.? This month I was perilously close to being out on the street. *Now* I might be forced to do the one thing that I dreaded most — call my mother. What if she tried to coerce me or even worse, force me to come home. She'd have been well within her rights. I wasn't even eighteen yet.

If *that* happened what would become of my apartment, my friends, my gigs, *my whole fucking life?* Come to think of it, what about my new couch and dresser?

As I was contemplating the sheer and utter stupidity of my actions, Herbie entered the lobby. He stood for a minute in silence, narrowing his eyes and squinting at me — then out it came.

"You're fired!!!!

He turned on his heels, then inexplicably spun around.

"Didn't you see me trying to wave the band in?" Herbie was hissing in a kind of controlled whisper. "Couldn't you see I was frantically trying to get your attention?"

He wasn't done yet.

"You, my friend, who's only played with this band a few short hours — are a *finagler.* You're the kind of person that tries to make every situation work to *your* advantage. Well, that's not going to happen, baby! I don't know *what* you did with Mingus, but with *me* you toe the line!

As he was engaged in his little object lesson, a few tears started to fall down my cheeks. Was I sorry? Not really. Was I stupid? Yes. Maybe those were tears of contrition for my own stupidity. Who knows? In any event, when Herbie saw those little rivulets of water trickling down, he softened up.

"O.K., look, I want you to make me a promise," Herbie said dampening his tone a bit. In the corner of my eye I could see one of the young honeys Herbie had previously hooked up with in the corner waiting for him. The cat was in a hurry. "I want you to promise *never ever* to do that again."

I dramatically raised my hand, palm up like I was swearing on a stack of bibles or becoming a boy scout.

"I promise."

"O.K. my friend. I'll see you tomorrow night, seven sharp in front of my building."

With that Herbie disappeared into a dark corner of the lobby and whisked away the little blond chick. I guess Mrs. Mann had split earlier that evening. In any event, I knew if I hung with the band for a while I'd get the scoop. I'd already heard a few rumors of shady little escapades that purportedly went on inside the Mann's marriage. Rumors usually traveled faster than the speed of light.

Soon I would know all.

++++

Later that night as I was trying to find a comfortable position on my couch, I started thinking about how lucky I was. Oh yeah, I did an uncool thing as far as Herbie was concerned but I really didn't have to pay very much penance. Well, maybe a few seconds of feeling uncomfortable but .... As a matter of fact, having Miles Davis notice me was worth all the bullshit I put myself through. I was inspired, not only by him and his band but by the possibility that someday, somehow, *I* could play some *real* music. Some live floating-through-space, muse whispering in your inner ear, kind of stuff.

On the other hand, perhaps I should have been thinking about my long-term welfare.

What if Herbie had lowered the boom. My rent was due next week. And there was a waiting list a mile long of people who wanted to move into my building. I could be out in the streets in two seconds flat.

Feeling destitute and penniless was not something I relished.

Maybe I should open a savings account. Then I could pick and choose my gigs as long as I had enough money in the bank. Of course that meant that I would have to stop my impulse buying, which I dug. What about that fringe jacket I had my eye on?

I quickly discarded that option.

What if I had a boyfriend, like my mom had who paid all the bills and was always forking over cash? Damn! *Where* did I come up with that one? How *disgusting.* Anyway who'd want a chick that was always studying Stravinsky scores, notating Bird solos and was too preoccupied to shave under her arms?

That one went into the trash.

What about a roommate?

I thought about that one for a long time. I couldn't see any immediate disadvantages. If both of us kept to our separate rooms and shared in the expenses, it could be cool. You could almost go out on Amsterdam Avenue with a begging bowl and come up with the amount of money it took to live in N.Y. — at least in my neighborhood, *if* you had a roommate.

That was it! Now I had a plan. My new roomie could watch the apartment while I was on the road, pick up my mail and keep things in order until I got back. Maybe she'd even like housework!!

I had made a decision. Suddenly my depression lifted. Wow, this was *soo* cool.

Time to lay back, relax, think of other things, do some of that ol' California mind-surfing.

After spacing out for a while, I found myself thinking about the upcoming gig Herbie had at some university. What was it called? Bernard? Barnyard? Whatever....

4

THE ROOMIE

For the last few months I'd been in a financial crunch. It was time to implement my plan to get a roommate. But how was I going to find one? I wanted someone with stability, who could share some of the financial burden.. She couldn't be a floater. I also needed someone who could accommodate *my* lifestyle. Tall order.

What I *didn't* want was someone crashin' around the pad at seven in the morning blaring their stupid clock radio, clinking coffee cups, whistling in the shower and waking me up. Uh uh. I didn't need any stormtrooper in jackboots thumpin' around in the A.M.

Hipness was another factor. Some teased-hair, polyester-sporting daytripper who sang Streisand songs, and thought Andre Previn *really* played would be *too* funky.

After ruminating a bit, I decided my roomie would have to be someone in the arts — a singer, dancer, or writer. Someone whose hours would conform to mine. *But* on the other hand, I needed someone who made enough bread to go halvsies with me on the rent and expenses.

I let it rest for a couple of hours. Then boom! A brilliant idea.

Right off the top of my head, I knew a few cats who had just broken up with their old ladies. Maybe I'd give *those* dudes a call and get some referrals. Any women who could tolerate going out with a jazz musician was probably mellow *and* self sufficient.

The first cat that came to mind was George Braith. I had heard through the grapevine that he'd just broken up with an artist who owned a coffee house. I'd even seen some of her paintings in a Mid-town exhibit: huge sperm-like shapes in primary colors with dots, squares and geometric designs floating around inside of them. Or maybe they weren't really sperm shapes. Perhaps they were teardrops or amoebas or something even farther out — who the hell knew?

On second thought, if she was a slob, she'd probably screw up the apartment with her her art supplies and crap. And if oil was her medium, she'd use turpentine. That shit gave me a headache. I'd probably have to take a lot of aspirin if she moved in.

And what if she sat on my *nearly* new couch with a painted-up, funky smock?

Cancel.

My next best bet was Herbie Hancock. He had just broken up with some dancer. We were rapping a few weeks ago at the Village Gate, and he had mentioned her. She sounded like she might be a contender.

I went to check my book. Groovy. I still had Herbie's number.

I was a little apprehensive about calling because he was an important dude and I didn't want him to think I was kissing ass.

Overriding my feelings I quickly dialed his number. After a few rings he picked up.

"Hello."

"Hi, may I please speak to Herbie Hancock?"

"This is Herbie, Who's this?"

"Jane Getz, man. I met you over at the Gate a couple of weeks ago and ...."

"Jane, yeah hey. What's happening?"

"Remember those chord voicings we were talking about. The ones with the major seventh in the root?"

"Yeah." Herbie said.

"Well I tried them. You know all the good shit." I'd hoped I was scoring points so I could broach the real subject. "We ought to get together sometime. We're practically neighbors."

Herbie cleared his throat.

"Yeah, well I'm pretty busy for the next couple of months but give me a call after that."

"Cool. Oh by the way. Remember that lady you told me about. What was her name? The one you just broke up with? I'm looking for a roommate. What's her situation?"

"Renee?" There was a big silence on the other end of the line. "Oh that's *unbelievable!* She *just* called me yesterday and said she had to move 'cause her landlord was about to give her a rent increase. Hold on a second. Let me get her number."

As I heard Herbie walk to the other side of the room, I tried to picture his crib. I knew he lived on Central Park West. And now I knew from the sound of his footsteps that he had hardwood floors. They were probably all buffed up to a high-gloss shine. He was pulling down some long bread from Miles. Maybe some day I would get a boss gig like that. A gig where all the cats in town envied me and tried to cop *my* shit. I superstitiously crossed my fingers as Herbie walked back to the phone.

"Hey man, I thought I misplaced her number but I found it in my old address book." Herbie paused. "Here it is: Trafalga nine-eight-four-two-seven. Give her a call. She stays up late. Yeah, she's a cool lady, maybe a bit of a complainer, but I think you two will get along very well."

"Thanks man. Later."

I hung up the phone and dialed Renee. I was excited. Maybe all my financial problems were about to fall by the wayside. But it wasn't only the bread. Lately I'd realized that I didn't have one female friend in all of New York. Yeah, and someone once told me that only hanging out with guys could make you more masculine. Shit, who wanted that!

By the time Renee picked up the phone (the girl had let it ring for at least seven times) I had already made up my mind. Unless there was something wild and bizarre about her — I mean something akin to having two heads — I was going to recruit her as my roomie. After rapping a few minutes, I suggested a face-to-face meeting so we could check each other out.

She liked that idea.

Renee and I agreed to get together at a funky old delicatessen in the East Village called Ratners. Musicians ate there because you could slurp a ton of mushroom-barley soup and stuff your face with all the rolls you could eat for a buck.

Upon arrival, I stood by the cash register until my eyes adjusted themselves to the dim lighting. Then I scanned the room looking for a chick with long dark hair, a white cotton blouse and a black mini. Renee was just coming from her waitressing gig.

Someone fitting that description was sitting in a corner booth.

She was sipping coffee and looking bored.

Without hesitation, I scurried across the pitted grey linoleum.

"Renee?"

"Yeah hi. You must be Jane." She had a rather low nasal voice — a voice that could easily modulate into a whine.

"Herbie told me a lot about you." I said. "All good."

"Really? Yeah, Herbie's a nice cat. Just not my cup of tea."

Mmm. I let that one slide.

Over the course of an hour or two, we drank coffee and rapped about out lives past and present. After discovering she liked Kahlil Gibran and Bill Evans, I thought it a safe bet to let her move in. Anyone that could quote from "The Prophet" ....

++++

I was surprised by Renee's lack of possessions. How could a bonafide chick only own two skirts (one of them being a black work-skirt) and three blouses? She didn't even fill up the cab when she moved in.

Cool. That meant I would have most of the closet space.

After observing her over the course of a week, I learned a few more things about her.

She was preoccupied with her weight, obsessively studying herself from all angles in her floor length propped-up cracked mirror. Though she was 5'6" and weighed 110 pounds, she was shooting for the perfect dancer's body — that of a twelve year old boy.

To lose those imaginary unwanted pounds, Renee tried to keep her eating down to a half a sandwich per day. When that failed, she ended up pillaging my food supply. One day she'd actually scarfed up a whole jar of my favorite kosher dills.

That was it!!

I rapidly put an end to that and made the first two shelves of the refrigerator off limits to starving dancers.

She was also a slob, but I couldn't throw any stones on that count.

The fact that she was a smartass was okay by me. I could sharpen *my* claws on her too. Besides, hanging with the cats required a certain aplomb in the "put-down" department.

Aside from all that minor stuff, she was nice enough.

She wasn't around much anyway due to her waitressing, modeling for art classes, and taking dance.

But though Renee put a lot of time into dancing, she admittedly wasn't good enough to become a professional dancer. Even weirder than that, she often told me she probably would never be good enough to become a pro.

I wondered why anyone would do *anything* if they knew they would never be able to reap any rewards, see some kind of payoff, or be remunerated in some way for their efforts. Was that *American?*

++++

Several weeks after Renee moved in, I got a call from Herbie Mann. There was a gig coming up at one Bernard, Barnyard — I didn't quite catch the name. It was a chance for me get out of town and make some pretty decent bread. Though playing with Herbie Mann wasn't really my bag, neither was starving.

The only drawback about going out of town was not being able to see Joe Chambers, a cute young drummer I was into. Now I would lose a couple of days. I didn't know how Joe felt, but I really had eyes for *him.*

Sometimes I'd lend him the key to my apartment so he could practice my piano while I was gigging. Oftentimes he was still there when I got back from my gig.

If he felt like hanging out, I'd put some Bartok or Stravinsky on the hi-fi. We'd check it out for a while, then discuss the harmonic moves the composer made. Sometimes Joe would even bring over the score to some particular concerto he wanted to listen to. We frequently went sailing into the wee small hours, rapping, comparing, critiquing, and analyzing.

I was hoping Joe would see how much we had in common. I'd only recently become familiar with the concept of "soulmates" but when I thought of Joe I was certain I'd found mine. Of course, being so young and inexperienced, I didn't have much in the way of feminine wiles. But I was hoping that after he got to know me, he would realize how perfect we were for each other.

I asked Renee — just to be on the safe side — if *she* was attracted to Joe, but every time I brought it up she simply said that black cats weren't her thing anymore. Uh, uh. Getting hooked up with one might hurt her parents. She was in the market for some tall dark Jewish guy with a steady job, and/or good career potential.

Shit, my mom didn't really care *who* I was with. Her only stipulation as to my choice of men, was that they either be gainfully employed, had a trust fund, or possessed a treasure chest.

Having eradicated the possibility of competition between my roomie and me I decided to have a key made for Joe. We weren't on romantic terms yet, but I was hoping.

++++

It didn't take long to pack. I had it down to a science. Everything I needed for a road trip was on a list, of which I had made three carbon copy duplicates. I'd just pack an item then check it off. Pack, check, pack, check.

After loading my bags up I gave Renee a set of instructions for the apartment, ran to the bank for a few extra *pesos* and wrote a short little note for Joe.

I sprayed it with perfume and left it on the piano.

Then I schlepped my suit-case down the block and around the corner and met Herbie and some other guys from the band in front of Herbie's Central Park West luxury crib.

When I caught sight of Herbie's shiny new car, I decided to ride with him. Yeah, his short was happenin' with its cushy leather seats, air conditioning and leg room.

Once we got on the open road, the ride was so smooth it felt like we were riding on marshmallows. I was groovin', leaning back-counting the telephone polls. I had almost fallen asleep when I had a flash.

Now I knew where we were going. The name of the university was Barnyard University... and ...Wait a minute!

Hold it ....

If the name of the college was *Barnyard U.* that would mean there were animals there. Now it was all making sense. We were going to a school of animal husbandry or something. Cool. I could just picture all the cute little animals: little baby cows, pigs, and horses. Wow! Perhaps they would have some llamas for variety. Weren't llamas considered livestock in South America?

I'd seen some llamas in a petting zoo once and thought they were adorable. This was going to be a very warm and fuzzy trip. Damn, maybe — if luck was smiling — I'd take a baby llama back to the Big Apple. I thought of all the ways I could smuggle a llama into a hotel. Then I leaned back in the seat, smiling and sinking into the lush upholstery.

I must have fallen asleep because the next thing I knew we were in a parking lot. About five carloads of musicians from Herbie's band had converged on the blacktop and were unloading their instruments. Herbie directed us to hurry and set up, because the school photographer wanted to take pictures of the band before the concert.

Since the piano was already on stage, I caught up with Herbie in front of the auditorium. I thought it would be cool to meet some of the kids and members of the faculty.

The president of the student body and a few campus big wigs came up to welcome us. They were excited to have us here. The student body prez — a big blonde cat who looked like a future farmer to me — strolled up with his academic cronies.

"Hi, I'm Carl Pullman, and I'd like to welcome you on behalf of the student body. *Please* let us know if there's *anything* we can do for you."

Herbie started to shake Carl's hand and speak but before he could do his flesh pumping routine *I* blurted out, *"I'd like to see the animals."*

What?

Everything stopped. Herbie's extended hand was suspended in mid-air as he whipped his head around. The kids looked puzzled.

"This chick is crazy!" Herbie hissed. His face had contorted into a frown. His mouth looked like an upside down half moon.

Now what did I do wrong? I was mystified as Herbie and Carl walked away leaving me standing there.

What the hell was wrong with being a farmer? Our ancestors were farmers. If being a farmer was a bad thing, then why did the 4-H Club come to our grammar school? I remembered how all the kids got to sit on this three-legged stool while they attempted to milk a cow. Sadly, no one really got any milk from the thing because it was just a demo cow — a cow, carted around to grammar schools, who didn't mind being touched, mauled, and manhandled by a bunch of second graders.

The incident puzzled me. What did Herbie have against animals?

I kinda forgot about it while we were giving the concert but later on when we were all packing up I went over to talk to Dave Pike and ran the incident by him.

"I don't know what happened man. I *just* asked them if I could see the animals. Pure and simple. What's so out about that?"

Dave suddenly stopped what he was doing and looked up, narrowing his eyes. "Why did you ask to see the animals?"

"Well isn't this Barnyard University?"

Dave broke up. He was laughing so hard he couldn't talk for a few minutes.

"No man," Dave finally said "It's not Barnyard, it's Barnard."

I started to laugh too.

++++

Right after the afternoon concert, we drove south about ninety five miles, to some Holiday Inn near Connecticut. We had another gig the next day in close proximity.

After a band pow-wow in the lobby, we all agreed to go to some fancy restaurant Herbie had read about in his gourmet digest.

I trotted up to my room to change.

I set my suitcase on the bed and pulled up some fancy silk pants that had an exotic multi-colored Indian pattern embossed on them. They were technically pajama bottoms, but no one but me knew it. The chick that had sold them to me swore that *those* particular pants could travel anywhere.

I slipped on the P.J.'s then decided to let my dark kinky hair go wild. I also put on an armful of jingling Indian bracelets and lined my eyes with kohl. I was making a statement. Looking at my exaggerated eye makeup, I decided you could either peg me as an exotic Indian dancer or a raccoon.

Giving myself the once over in the full length mirror in the bathroom, I confidently walked out to the parking lot to meet the band. A couple of the cats whistled. Yep, I looked pretty foxy.

Not wanting to ride with Herbie tonight for obvious reasons, I opted to ride in a car jammed with five yammering cats. Since I was a bit claustrophobic it was not something I relished. If being crammed into the car like a sardine wasn't bad enough, as soon as we hit the road, someone started passing a joint around. I smoked occasionally, but only when I was back at the crib. Being out in the world stoned was too much for me.

While the rest of the cats were tokin' I stuck my head out of the window so I wouldn't get a contact high. By the time we reached the restaurant, my artfully messy hair had turned into a frenzied mop. Now I *really* looked freaky. But the cats were so wasted by the time they got out of the car no one noticed.

Inside the restaurant we all stood around in a dark little alcove, waiting for the maître d' to show us to our table. After a few minutes some stuffed shirt in a tux appeared. As he was walking toward us, he eyeballed me. The cat had a weird expression on his face.

"Are you the Herbie Mann Party?" the penguin inquired, still eyeing me suspiciously.

"That's us." Herbie said impatiently.

"I put three tables together so everyone in your party can sit together...ah, but there's only one thing..." the maître d' said. "We don't allow pants in *this* establishment. I'm sorry but the lady will have to go home and change."

Before Herbie could respond, I looked the stuffed shirt in the eye and said in my best East Indian accent, "Oh but I am noot frum yer country. Thees ees myee native dress. lee kant change unless I flyee bock to Calcutta to get myee sari."

The guy in the penguin suit first looked at Herbie, then eyeballed the rest of the cats in the band. No one said anything. There was complete silence. For a few seconds the maître d' looked confused, then, since economics undoubtedly superseded house rules, he silently ushered us to our tables.

Now Herbie was *really* mad at me. He deliberately waited until I sat down, then seated himself at the opposite end of the table.

It was just speculation, but I guessed if I continued in his band much longer, he would probably wind up with ulcers or high blood pressure or some goofy psychological condition.

Reflecting on the day's happenings I felt sad. Perhaps this was the last gig I would play with Herbie's band. Why did I have to be so "up front" with everything.

I was sure that tonight's little incident was the third strike.

++++

Immediately following our afternoon gig, we drove straight through to New York. I arrived home about ten in the evening. I was bone tired.

The cats dropped me off in front of my building and I literally raced up the front stairs. I just wanted to unload my stuff and cool out.

Walking down the outside hallway to my crib, I heard someone plunking down some chords on my piano. Since Joe was the only other one besides me and Renee with a key, I figured it was him. After obsessing over the cat for the last several days, it seemed almost anticlimactic to see him in person. But what the hell. The universe didn't run on *my* time or for *my* convenience.

I stood at the door gathering my wits and fumbling around for my key. I finally felt the jagged metal key edge at the bottom of my purse and stuck it in the lock.

As I opened the door, Joe turned around and stared at me.

"Joe, what do you want in your coffee?" Someone yelled from the kitchen.

I recognized Renee's low whiny voice.

Huh?

Why wasn't Renee waitressing tonight?

Renee peaked her head outside of the kitchen door to make sure Joe had heard her.

The girls hair was kind of wild and tangled. Then I noticed she was only wearing a bathrobe.

"Hi Renee," I said, feeling a bit uncomfortable and not knowing what to think.

"Oh hi Jane," Renee said nervously. "I had a little cold today, so I decided to stay home and rest. Joe *just* got here a half an hour ago. Hey ya want some coffee?"

"Yeah, pour me a cup." I said trying to remain unaffected by the scene.

I set my bags down and went over to the piano and put my hand on Joe's shoulder in kind of a friendly gesture. He didn't respond. He continued playing for a while, *then* he turned around.

"So, how was your trip, man?"

Now I didn't mind when cats in the band called me man, but why did Joe have to call me that? I momentarily started to lose it.

Then I realized I was tired and cranky. Okay. Maybe I wasn't reading things right.

Renee exited the kitchen carrying a couple of cups of Java. After setting them down on the little orange crate near the piano, she went back into the kitchen to get herself a cup.

After rattling around the little cubby-hole and shutting a few cabinets, she came out of the kitchen again with her coffee mug. Looking straight ahead (as if she had blinders on) she walked through the living room to her bedroom and shut the door. I thought I saw Joe look up but ....

Joe, completely forgetting the question he had asked me, took a perfunctory sip of coffee then banged on my piano again. After a few uninspired licks, he excused himself.

"Hey man, tell Renee goodbye for me." he said offhandedly.

He headed for the door, not bothering to look behind him.

After Joe left, I tapped on the bedroom door.

"Renee, are you okay?"

"Oh yeah come on in."

"Why did Joe split so soon?" I asked.

"Oh I don't know." Renee said, making a point of stretching her neck and shoulders. "I was thinking of going to Baltimore this weekend to see my parents, but I can't get rid of this cold. I don't want to give it to them. When old people get sick, they can get real sick."

"Wow, Renee, it's pretty inspiring the way you treat your folks."

"Yeah I know." Renee said. "It's just too bad *you* don't have anyone *you're* related to on this coast."

Renee made that statement like she had one up on me.

"Oh I *do* have some relatives here on the east coast," I lied. "I just haven't looked them up yet."

"Well ya better hook it up soon. Yeah. I'm holding my breath."

Fuck. What was happening? This conversation was turning nasty. Joe left abruptly for no reason. What was happening? I was starting to feel like an intruder.

Well, this chick wasn't going to top *me!*

I ran to the phone book and looked up the name Getz. There were about twenty or so of them. I wrote the first five numbers down then ran to the front room, picked up the phone and dialed the first name on my list. The phone rang about five times, then a man with a deep rich voice picked up.

"Hello."

"Hi, may I please speak to Alden Getz."

"This is Alden."

"Hi Alden. This is Jane Getz and I wonder if I'm —"

"Are you Marvin's daughter?

Bingo!!

"Yes." Now my heart was pounding. This was *more* than luck.

"Oh my God." Alden gasped. "I'm Marvin's first cousin. How *are* you? I saw you when you were about two years old — many years ago in California. Are you in New York?"

"Yeah I'm calling from 91st Street." I said excitedly. Yes Renee, I mused, I *do* have relatives on this coast and closer then Baltimore I might add.

"Well Jane, we'd certainly *love* to see you. I bet we're right across the park from you. We live on 81st and Park Avenue.

Wait a minute, let me get Harriet." Alden put his hand over the receiver while he excitedly summoned his wife.

"Hi Jane," Harriet said. "I'm really anxious to meet you. Alden has spoken about your dad many times. We were very sorry to hear he passed away a few years ago. Anyway, we'd love you to come over for dinner tomorrow night. Is six okay for you?"

"Perfect." I said silently congratulating myself.

"I know it's kind of early," Harriet continued, "but Alden starts to fade around ten. That'll give you guys plenty of time to catch up on some family history and meet our son Daren. Anyway, let me give you back to Alden. See ya tomorrow night, sweetie."

Harriet handed the phone back to Alden and we confirmed the time and place, then said our goodbyes. I suddenly felt pretty good. Apparently my family *wasn't* limited to malcontents or nehr-do-wells. This call had broadened the vistas for my future.

I hurriedly put the phone in it's cradle and ran back to Renee's room.

"Hey, Renee," I said blithely. I've got a dinner date on Park Ave. tomorrow. A-huh. I know I *should* have called them sooner, but better late than never," I chortled.

Renee finally looked up from her book. She was probably reading another biography about a Russian Dancer that had defected from the good old U.S.S.R. Some pasty faced, stringy-haired egomaniac that was making big bucks from leaping, twirling, and brooding.

"You're so juvenile," Renee sniffed, rolling her eyes.

I watched her go into her Miss Sophisticate routine, then something hit me. Her orbs kinda looked like she had laminated them with frosted blue eye shadow. Damn! What exactly was she doing with all that eyeshadow on if she was sick in bed all day?

I was just about to ask her why all the eye makeup, when she conveniently yawned, informing me she needed her beauty rest.

Now I already knew from the Mingus experience that I was prone to jumping to conclusions. So I filed the little tidbits of info rattling around in my brain away. Time will tell, I thought.

++++

That night I fell into a fitful slumber, dreaming about, handsome young drummers, rich relatives, a ballet dancer, and a tiny little Cuban titmouse that played conga drums. Sometimes when you sleep, weird things make perfect sense.

5

MY NEW FAMILY

It felt good to have a New York family. So what if I looked them up in the telephone book? There were worse ways to meet people — like at funerals and lawyers' offices.

Come to think of it, my immediate family was such an antisocial lot, the phone book probably *was* my best available source of connecting with other family members.

As the cab sped through Central park, I tried to imagine what cousin Alden looked like. Maybe he was tall and dark with an aquiline nose like my dad. After all, they *were* first cousins.

Looking like my dad wouldn't be half bad. Dad had been the proverbial ladies man. The magnetic, eye catcher from Texas. When I was a little girl, I got a kick out of my mother's girlfriends always flirting with him. They'd walk up real close to my old man, inhale their cigarettes, then seductively let out a narrow stream of smoke that caressed his face. Or they'd suck in their tummies, lean their heads back and suggestively put their hands on their hips. Dad once -said they were trying to copy Rita Hay worth.

I wondered what seductress the women of today could emulate?

I tried to lean back and relax, but I was too antsy. Besides the cab had a peculiar odor. What *was* it? Almost like the last passenger had been on a bender, then taken a bath in Old Spice. Whew!

By the time we pulled up to my cousin's building on 85th and Park Avenue, I was ready. I handed the cabbie the exact fare plus a healthy tip. Before he could thank me, I sprinted up to the entrance of this huge white stone building, with ornate designs and scary looking gargoyles on the facade. The building might as well have had a sign on it that said "old money." Everything was meticulous and polished: the windows, the carpeted entryway, the wrought-iron adornments on the outside of the huge glass double doors. Even the gigantic potted plants on both sides of the front door were green and thriving — like some professional plant doctor was attending to them.

I gave my name to the doorman, a huge ruddy fellow with gold braided tassels exploding off his shoulders, and waited for him to ring the Getz's. After what seemed like an eternity, he directed me down the hallway and pointed to the elevator.

It was one of those elevators with benches in it. I imagined if you were old and rich, it would probably be cool to sit down while you were riding up to your floor.

I stood up.

Four floors later, I walked into a square little alcove with two doors opposite each other. One of them was open slightly. As I looked in that direction, a smiling man with arms outstretched, appeared.

"Hi darling," Cousin Alden said giving me the big squeeze. "It's so wonderful to see you!"

The man hugging me was not exactly handsome. In fact, he looked nothing like my father. Alden had a ruddy complexion, a bulbous nose and thinning sandy hair, but he also had something more valuable than looks. He had real charisma plus a kind of authority that only comes from making your own way in the world.

Standing right behind him was his wife Harriet, who was a thin waif-like woman who appeared to be somehow luminescent. She had a laugh like tinkling bells.

So these were my fairy-godparents.

Checking out their crib was like being ushered into a magic kingdom. Sure, I had seen people with cool pads, but *this* was different. This was fucking *over the top.*

People that lived in places like this knew something I didn't. Those folks had Long Bread. *Their* money made money even when they were sleeping. My upstairs neighbor, Jerome Richardson, with his wall to wall carpeting and spiffy dinette set, seemed like a piker now.

My eyes were big as saucers as I surveyed the cavernous living room, formal dining room, three enormous guest bedrooms, huge master suite, wood paneled den, ultra-modern kitchen, and utility room with maids quarters attached.

Besides an incredible amount of space, they had a wealth of costly art treasures. Jackson Pollack graced one wall, a Caulder mobile artfully bobbed near the front door while a canvas of Byzantine angels flew serenely above their living room fireplace. If this wasn't cool ....

After touring their digs, we retreated to the dining room and sat down to a lowfat meal. The maid entered with a platter full of chicken and a pot of steaming vegetables.

"I hope you like Salsa Chicken, Jane." Alden said. "This is one of Lena's specialties. She skins the chicken breast and bastes it with salsa. Harriet and I try to watch our calories and fat intake."

"I'm sure I'll like it," I said cutting the breast into little squares and remembering the huge steak with the one inch border of fat I had eaten the other day.

As I conversed with them, I tried to watch my P's and Q's. I was trying to appear knowledgeable, albeit in a hip way. I didn't want to sound like one of the weird street cats I frequently hung out with. The cats with strange smelling cigarettes you had to keep relighting and bottles of Ripple tucked away in the pockets of their trench coats.

While we were rapping, my six year old cousin, Darin, sat there with a terribly serious face. I noticed he bore a distinct resemblance to my dad. The little boy had beautiful olive skin and black hair — just like dad. It made me feel sad and proud at the same time.

As the night wore on, I felt we were all linked together somehow. Alden and Harriet felt the connection too. I'd catch Alden looking at me nostalgically like he was remembering my father. In fact, he told me a lot of things about Dad I never knew. Dad had once been a great tennis player and had thought about becoming a pro. He also had been president of his fraternity in college.

Alden was modest about his own life. Though he was a man of high accomplishment (he'd once owned a newspaper and now had an advertising agency) he was not a self promoter. After quickly glossing over his present endeavors, Alden asked me about mine.

I downplayed the drugs, the wacky hours, and the undisciplined activities. Instead, I concentrated on the unique, contributions the cats I knew were making to twentieth century music.

I tried to explain to my cousins that I was part of a relatively new American art form called jazz. In fact, since I had already played with cats like Charlie Mingus and Herbie Mann, I was in on the ground floor. The Getz's turned on their high beams when I mention a few big names. Nope, they weren't beyond being impressed.

By the end of the evening, Alden and Harriet, fascinated with my little Odyssey, wanted to come and hear me. I promised we would keep in touch and that I'd inform them next time I played somewhere close.

I left that night loaded down with a shopping bag full of designer clothes, a few new editions from their book advertising agency, and big bag of biscuits from some trendy bakery on the upper East Side.

++++

There was a note on my piano when I got back to the crib. Herbie Mann had called. Strange. I was certain he would never hire me again. Maybe he was a glutton for punishment.

It was late so I decided to return his call in the morning.

I was really hoping Joe would be there when I got home, but he wasn't.

I wanted to practice, but rapping with relatives and trying to speak the King's English all night took a lot of energy. I lay down on my lumpy couch/bed and started cutting Zzz's almost immediately.

Renee was up early. As she walked through the living room to the bathroom, I noticed she hadn't washed her face before she went to bed. Her ugly blue eyeshadow was still on.

"Ya must've had a late night last night," I said.

"No such luck," Renee replied. "I just had a beer with a friend."

"Oh yeah! what was the cat's name?"

"Oh, no one *you'd* know," she said noncommittally. "Ya better call Herbie Mann. He sounded anxious to get in touch with you."

"Cat's anxious for me to give him a nervous breakdown!" I joked.

Renee closed the bathroom door and fired up the shower.

I dialed up Herbie.

Minutes later, I wrote a date on my calendar. Next week this time *I'd* be in Chicago having a blast. We were playing the London House! I'd heard it was a stuffy little steakhouse that usually featured trio's like Marian McPartland or Ahmad Jamal. Strictly cocktail jazz. To me, it sounded like one of those ultra expensive places where you'd take a hot first date, an important client, or someone you just wanted to put some moves on. But what the hell! A gig was a gig and I was glad to be working.

I padded into the kitchen where Renee was puttering around and told her the scoop. Then I showed her all the loot I had gotten from my relatives.

"Renee, I'm sure some of this shit is too big for me. You're welcome to try it on if it doesn't fit me".

"Thanks," Renee said, looking rather bored at the whole proposition. "Oh by the way, Herbie Hancock's having a party this weekend. Wanna go?"

"Sure, if I'm not working."

++++

That afternoon I decided to do something I swore I would never do — straighten my hair. I went to a beauty shop that was recommended by a waitress/friend of mine named Wynona. She was light skinned and had fine kinky hair like mine. Men were always hitting on her and I figured that her luxurious, glossy straight hair played a part in upping her desirability quotient.

I was a little skittish when I first entered the beauty shop, but after meeting the beautician, I calmed down. She seemed knowledgeable about the stuff she was about to use on me, so I let her brush out my curly do and douse my hair with some foul smelling chemicals. About five minutes later — and after much coughing and wheezing on my part — she rinsed the evil smelling stuff off, combed out my hair, and snipped a few inches off. She then handed me a mirror.

"Whaddya think, darlin'?"

I was blown away.

I studied myself from different angles.

"Man, I've never had silky straight hair before. I look so...so normal. This is un-fucking-real. You did a great job. Yeah ... dynamite!"

I handed Wynona a big tip.

When I got home, I heard Renee puttering around in the kitchen.

I tiptoed across the living room floor and silently stood in the doorframe.

"Yikes!" Renee said looking up. "What on *earth* did you do to your hair. That length makes your face look so round. In fact, you kinda look like the full moon. Shit, now I'm gonna have to start calling you Moonface." Miss Smartass laughed.

"Well Renee, you're just jealous 'cause I got a lot of shit going. I'm only seventeen and I'm already playing with some of the heavies. You're four years older and you've never even been in an *amateur* ballet let alone the Bolshoi or some crap like that."

Renee's face turned an angry shade of red.

She half sneered. "Yeah, well don't get so goddam cocky with me. I could tell you something that would level you — take all the wind out of *your* little sails, but guess what? I'm savin' it for another day." Renee said testily.

Renee plodded across the floor to her bedroom.

"When you tour Russia," I shouted to Renee, "give the Volga Boatman my regards."

"Oh shut up little dirge." Renee screamed back.

Now *that* was clever. Renee had bested me in the garbage hurling department.

I obsessively looked in the mirror for a few days, cursing my moon face, 'till some bass player told me what a hot little number I was.

Though the tension dissipated, I was left wondering what secret Renee was keeping from me. The chick sounded like she had some live ammunition.

++++

I was ready for Herbie Hancock's big to-do. I had on some black tight pants and boots, and an orange see-through blouse. I looked in what had once been a floor-length mirror, but now was a large jagged propped-up piece of glass to check out my locks.

Renee rolled her eyes. "Why doncha just buy a new mirror? Someone as vain as you deserves a mirror that's intact."

"Well, I wouldn't have run into the damn thing if *you* hadn't'a moved it! Anyway *you're* the one who watches herself for hours doing leg lifts!"

"Well you should have looked where you were going Miss Putt-Putt" Renee sniffed, then looked up.

"Is *that* what you're wearing?" She said.

"Yeah man. It's the sixties. Get hip to it!" Renee was a fashion zombie. Why was she wearing that floor-length black dress she had pilfered from Aunt Harriet's grab bag. It was something you'd strut around in if you were forty or fifty.

I guffawed and smoothed down an unwieldy strand of hair. Suddenly, I heard a key in the door.

I trotted out to the living room.

"Hey man, what's up?" Joe said walking over to the piano.

"Oh, me and Renee are going to Herbie Hancock's party."

"I know. Renee told me. I might catch y'all later."

I was trying to do a fluttery little thing with my eyes but Joe didn't notice. In fact, he didn't even notice my new straight hair or tight black pants.

However, he *did* notice when Renee walked into the middle of the room.

Joe whistled under his breath.

Renee smugly smiled and licked her lips, seductively sashaying to the door in her dowager dress.

What the hell was up?

++++

Herbie's party was a big fucking deal. He had a spread with Danish crackers and at least five different kinds of smelly cheeses. There was also a big cauldron of pink punch and for the more discriminating souls, a table of fine French wines.

I stood by the cheese platter stuffing my face until I realized that every time I chucked down a hunk of that yellow crap my hips were expanding and my face was getting even rounder.

Time to mingle.

Tony Williams was just walking in the door. He was *soo* thin and gangly he looked about fifteen. His little moustache made him look younger, not older as *he* imagined.

I walked up to him.

'"Hey man. What's up?" I was hoping he'd remember me from the Village Gate.

"Man, I'm cool," he said tonelessly. Then he looked over my head and spotting someone more influential, loped away.

The guy in the corner, who had a head like a pool ball, was standing alone so I walked slowly toward him. Just as I was about to introduce myself, he looked past me and waved to someone. Later I found out *his* name was George Avakian. He managed Charles Lloyd.

I was batting 0 for 2. I decided to make one last ditch effort. I walked up to this bass player I knew from D.C. named Mickey.

"Hey Mickey, what's shakin?"

Mickey narrowed his eyes trying to figure out who I was.

"Oh man I didn't recognize you with your hair so short and straight," Mickey finally said. "Shit, I was wondering, do you know where I can get some blow? I got this chick back at the pad. Tonight I'm gonna party! Oh yeah, *partee* baby."

"Sorry man, I can't help you." I said. I could see Mickey's limited attention span had been depleted, so I walked away. Shit, all the cats were acting like a bunch of preening jazz peacocks.

After standing alone for a few more minutes, I decided to take a tour of Herbie's place. The cat had glossy hardwood floors, a Steinway Grand in the living room, and a sparsely furnished bedroom. Very Zen.

By this time it was apparent that no one was clamoring to meet meet me so I looked for Herbie and Renee. They weren't in the immediate vicinity so I split.

I was home in a matter of minutes.

Joe was practicing some pentatonic-sounding stuff. I stood in back of him, waiting until he finished polishing off his riff. He took his sweet time.

"Man, you weren't gone very long," Joe said, casually turning around. "You get bored or something?"

"Shit, there was nothin' happenin', "I said once again batting my eyelashes at him.

"Something in your eye, man?"

"No," I said pretending I didn't know what I'd just done.

"Ya wanna go to the cafeteria on Amsterdam and have some dinner?" Joe said. Now *that* was totally unexpected.

I'd already eaten, but I wasn't going to miss this chance to go out with the cat I had a jones for.

"Sure. Oh, could you help me on with my coat?"

Joe picked my coat up from the couch and held it while I wriggled in to it. This was starting to feel like a real date. Then my mind leaped ahead. For just a second I pictured myself in a long flowing white gown and Joe in a rented tux, standing at an alter in some huge edifice. I caught myself before the fantasy could go any further.

I grabbed Joe's arm in a show of solidarity and walked down the front steps. We had almost reached the bottom when this cat by the name of Dog walked up. Dog *was* an absolute dog. The dude had a stable of hookers, ran numbers, and boosted shit right and left. But since he was a neighbor, I always talked to him.

"Hey! What jou cats into?" Dog gave me the once over, then stuck his hand out for Joe to shake.

"Oh, nothin'," I said quickly, trying to end the exchange before it got started.

"You still workin' with ... what's that cat's name... Herbie Mann?"

"Yeah, I'm goin' out of town with him next week." I said hurriedly. "Anyway, we're on our way to this thing. Catch ya later."

With that I tugged at Joe's arm and we were off.

"Man, I hate that cat." Joe whispered as we walked away.

"Yeah, but there's no possible way that cat's going to do either of us any damage," I said smugly. "I got iron gates on my back window and two double locks on my door."

Famous last words.

As for our little outing, nothing — as usual — happened. The date was another big zero. Zip! The cat even had the nerve to ask me to pay for my own salad!!

++++

Before I left for Chicago, I made an impulse buy.

Walking by an appliance store on Amsterdam Ave., I saw a huge color T.V. in the window.

I stood there watching this beautiful young model being interviewed. I recognized the chick from the fashion magazines. Jean Shrimpton. She was *much* cooler than Twiggy — another British import. She was part of the new Rock culture.

As I continued watching,, I realized there were other worlds, apart from the jazz world that I hadn't explored.

Sometimes I felt connected to the jazz world and at other times I felt like some kind of alien voyeur who was allowed to witness the musical festivities but not participate. No matter how hard I tried, I could not be an old black man. Hell, I couldn't even be black and the man part — well forget it. Anyway, I had enough testosterone to be an aggressive player. That's all I needed. And fortunately, most of the cats thought I had enough talent to take me past all the superficial differences.

The world of jazz was an insular place — a little musical cubby hole, a sonic crawl space, an intellectual niche. At times, I liked being in a safe sequestered domain, free from the outside influences of loud thrumming guitars, piano players pounding out clunky triads and overamped, gravel voiced vocalists screaming inane rhymes and obscenities into the mike.

Yeah, I dug the jazz world, *but* I still had the feeling there were other things out there. If I was snobby about the music I played (as were most jazzers), I was also curious about some of the other musical forms that were emerging. In fact, I had heard a few things that I actually dug.

I wanted to hear them again — and see them.

I needed a T.V.

So I went into the store and worked out a deal on a nearly new, black and white, sixteen inch set.

That afternoon they delivered my T.V. I noticed that the old man who sold me the thing tacked on another twenty five bucks for delivery. But what the hell. I still had a few days to watch the damn thing before I went to the Windy City.

For the next two days I sat there glued to the T.V. set. I couldn't even pack without running back into the living room to check out some stupid-assed program.

By the time I left for the airport, I had dark blue circles under my eyes from watching the tube.

As we boarded the plane, I looked at my seat number. I was sitting next to Potato Valdez. Now I knew — at least for the next few hours — I wasn't going to get *any* sleep. The Cubano chatterbox would be assaulting my ears, ranting and raving about Castro and how life was before the Communistas took over. Or, for a change of pace, extolling the virtues of Cuban cuisine.

Trying to understand what Potato was saying took every ounce of my energy.

Good guess! As the plane took off, Potato expounded non-stop on the superior diet the Cubans had. Nothing, he said could beat the nutritional value of red beans and rice. And there was no equal to olive oil for keeping your innards lubricated and your muscles hard.

"Yust feel how hard." Potato pointed to his stomach. He wanted me to punch him.

I playfully, gave him a little jab.

"No Yane — harder!!"

I punched him a bit harder. His little abdomen was like a brick wall. At that moment I realized that no matter how hard I punched the dude I could never hurt him.

"Wow man, that's fuckin' unbelievable" I said. "Why don't you make us all a big dinner while we're in Chicago. I really gotta taste some of that Cuban shit you keep bragging about. I'm sure, Herbie'll have a kitchen in his crib!"

At my suggestion, Potato started to beam. I could tell, the little cat was now planning the bash of the century. He was *so* up that he started to speak rapidly in Spanish.

To my ears, Potato sounded like a chicken squawking in gibberish.

For the rest of the plane ride Potato frantically planned the menu for his big Chicago soiree.

My ears were ringing when the plane touched down. I was ready for a long nap. Herbie Mann had some record exec pick him up while the rest of us cabbed it. A short time later we all checked into our home away from home — a twenty three story hotel called the Delaware. It was fairly upscale, about a mile from the gig.

After checking out the gig time, I went up to my room. Very groovy. It was a two room suite complete with full-length mirror in the bathroom. I put my bags down and bounced on the bed. Firm but not too firm.

Naptime.

I was deep in a dream when the phone rang. It was Herbie. He told me we were having a sound check in an hour and to wear or bring with me my gig clothes because we weren't coming back to the hotel. I got dressed because I hated schlepping stuff around.

That night, I wore a new short peach minidress and combed my newly straightened hair around my face. I admired myself in the mirror. If I was taller maybe I could have been a model. My new hair gave me that extra fashion bonus. Who the hell cared *what* my stupid roommate thought?!

++++

The London house was one of those listen-while-you-eat places. All the tables were facing the bandstand. There was also a ring of tables that were right up against the stage, the same height as the bandstand. If one of the customers was a drag, you could actually walk off the bandstand, and step right onto his table. Mashed potatoes on your shoes weren't half as bad as dogshit. But *I* had to be extra careful. Herbie didn't like anything spontaneous except a piano solo, coming from *moi*.

We quickly got through our sound check, skating through a few bars of "Summertime." The sound guy, a cat with frizzy hair and a bald spot adjusted a few mikes then split.

Sound check over, the band retreated to a little burger joint around the corner. I sat next to Bruno Carr who told a few lame jokes, then stared off into space until it was time to go.

I really didn't care if anyone talked to me or not. I was busy breathing in the hickory smoke and obsessing on Joe. I felt a twinge of anxiety every time I thought about him, but I couldn't stop.

When we got back to the London House it was just about time to hit.

I walked up to the bandstand and glanced down. Seated directly to the side of me and in the front row were two waspy middle-aged businessmen. "Can we buy you a drink?" One of them said as I slid across the piano bench.

Damn! We hadn't even started yet and those fuckin' day trippers were bugging me.

Ignoring them I put my music in order and stared straight ahead.

Herbie counted off "Summertime."

All during Dave Pike's high energy solo, to Potato's polyrythmic explorations, and on to Herbie's jocular flute cadenza, the two suits in the front row rapped. And to make matters worse when the song ended, they cheered, whistled, and screamed "Bravo" — like they *had* been listening.

Damn! What right did *they* have to applaud? I turned around and gave them a cold stare, but they were oblivious to me. Then I thought of all the people who had lived and died for jazz. Charlie Parker, Clifford Brown, Billie Holiday, Fats Navarro ... the list went on and on.

The two suits were pissing me off. *Royally.*

All through the set they talked above the music, clinked their glasses, carelessly dropped their utensils on their plates, and kept shouting for the waitress.

It was as irritating as having a fly continually buzzing around your face at a picnic. No, on second thought, they were *more* irritating.

By now I was infuriated.

Those rubes even yammered away during soft ballads, and bass solos. I wanted them to know, that they couldn't get away with it, but if I said anything ....

At the end of the set I waited until Herbie's back was turned, then I stepped on their table, put my hands on my hips — careful not to step in their food — and jumped off unto the floor. A couple of cats in the band saw me, rolled their eyes and laughed.

At first the two squares looked puzzled, then one of them got an angry look on his face.

I was really thinking of flipping them the bird but at the last minute I aborted the gesture. Why? Because of Alden and Harriet. I now figured I was part of a distinguished family and though I could still be a little bad, I couldn't be *that* bad.

Aside from my newfound considerations, I was *still* seventeen. So as an afterthought I flipped them the bird when they weren't looking.

No harm, no foul.

By the next set, the noxious suits had split. The rest of the night was a piece of cake. As good as *that* gig could get anyway.

The next day Mark Weinstein (the trombone player) called me and told me Diz was in town and Kenny Barron (his piano player) was staying at our hotel. I'd met Kenny when I was playing with Blue Mitchell. We both promised we'd get together if we had the chance.

I buzzed his room.

"Hey Kenny! Getz here. I'm in room 1106. Wanna get together?"

"Sure. We kin do that. Do you know where there's a piano?"

"Yeah, there's one in the lounge downstairs. I already checked it out with the guy at the desk."

"You're on man. I'll meet you in the lobby in a half an hour."

"See ya."

We wiled away the afternoon showing each other licks, talking philosophy and telling war stories. Kenny gave me the scoop on working for Diz and I rapped a little about gigging with Mingus. The bar didn't open until late afternoon so we hung until then. Then we decided to grab a bite around the corner at some burger joint.

About three bites into my chiliburger I checked my watch.

Oh, no! I was in trouble. I had almost forgotten, tonight was Friday, which meant we were starting an hour earlier. I apologized to Kenny and excused myself. I was supposed to meet the guys in the lobby in fifteen minutes. I had to get my ass in gear!

Back in the room, I put on a black pantsuit, dabbed on some lipstick, and ran a comb through my hair.

Putting the comb down I noticed a big clump of hair in it. I ran it through my hair a second time to see if my locks were *really* coming out.

Shit!! An even bigger clump came out. To make sure this wasn't a fluke, I ran the comb through my hair again.

Handfuls of the stuff were coming out. My silky tresses were starting to make little brown pools on the gold carpeting. Now there was a big bald spot in back.

I glanced around at the clock. Dammit! Three minutes left.

Deftly wetting all my hair down I put the pathetic little clump of hair in front in a pony tail to hide the bald spot. Then I grabbed my purse and ran to the elevator.

Screw straight hair! I felt around to the tragic little tail at the back of my head and vowed I would never do anything unnatural to my hair again.

Down in the lobby, a few of the guys made jokes about my *new look*. I held my tongue. It was okay to look like a skinned rat, 'cause hair grows back. This was just a temporary style setback. I decided my mantra for the evening would be: hair grows back, hair grows back, hair grows ....

But when I got to the gig I temporarily forgot about my diminishing tresses. The guys were all abuzz about the bash Potato was throwing. Oh yeah, tomorrow night, the little Cuban was serving up the "feast to end all feasts." As per my suggestion, it was being held in Herbie's room.

I wondered if Herbie would invite a couple of young chicks to the soiree. That seemed to be his thing. I had heard from Mark, the trombone player, that Herbie and his wife had some kind of financial arrangement going. Mark went as far as speculating that they had adopted their kids to get a tax write-off. Now *that* was hard to believe. But since I'd found my relatives through the phone book, I conceded anything was possible.

Well, whatever Herbie was doing, he was doing *something* right.

But so was I. Herbie hadn't fired, busted, or been mad at me for a whole week now. Tonight was especially cool. The music sounded like it was supposed to. I didn't miss any repeats or coda signs, didn't spill any drinks on the piano nor did any drunks slobber on my threads. Things were copacetic. Still....

It was like a cloudless day in a horror movie. You knew that something *very bad* was lurking beneath the serene blue sky and the placid scenery.

++++

Before we left, Potato made me promise I'd come to his party early.

"Me show Yane how cook." He said grinning ear to ear, showing his perfect pearly whites."

The next day I was still in a weird space. I got up early and walked around the neighborhood hoping to shake the feeling. The hotel was surrounded on one side by a vacant lot and on the other side by a few old brick buildings, housing mom and pop stores. After aimlessly roaming around, I went back to my room to watch the tube. Still, the feeling lingered.

That afternoon, I got ready for Potato's shindig. After trying on a few outfits, I decided on some tight paisley pants and a long straight yellow sweater. I slicked my hair back, opting to put on some ultra dramatic eye makeup. Since I *had* to wear my hair back, I thought I'd try to accentuate my eyes more.

I gave myself the once over in the full length mirror then went up to Herbie's crib.

As I walked toward Herbie's room, I could hear a few of the guys laughing and partying.

I knocked loudly. Potato answered.

"Ees Yane. Jou come in keechin."

As I walked in the door, my senses were assaulted by the strongest garlic smell ever. That smell was also infused with a red-peppery kind of aroma that burned your nose. Strong shit.

Of course, Potato had an iron constitution. Now it all made sense! Anyone that could eat food *that* spicy and live would have to have guts of corrugated steel.

Entering the kitchen, my eyes started to water.

"Oh Potato," I lied, "this chow looks good enough to eat, man."

"Ees delicion. Jou taste."

Potato stuck a spoonful of spicy black beans in my mouth. They were *so* hot, I immediately started to hiccup. Then my system went haywire. About every three seconds I made this loud gasp-like hiccuping sound. I was also gulping air for dear life. I quickly left the kitchen, hoping Potato's feelings weren't hurt. As I entered the living room, everyone turned and eyeballed me. All conversation ceased.

Herbie strode out of the bathroom to investigate. The cat wasn't wearing a shirt. I looked at his physique. What was wrong with this picture?

It hit me.

Herbie had hair covering his whole chest area *and* his upper back. *Very* thick hair. In fact, you couldn't just say the cat had a lot of body hair. Uh uh. *That* dude had a pelt.

I started to laugh. Now I was hiccuping, gulping air, and laughing hysterically.

It was the kind of nervous laughter that sometimes takes place at funerals, operas, and graduations. Strictly involuntary.

Herbie didn't have to say anything. I just knew from the look he gave me, he had had it with *my* sorry ass.

This time it was for good.

I had blown it.

Why couldn't I just shut up like the rest of the cats.

Sure, Potato's dinner party had been a good idea — in theory. I ended up eating a plate of plain rice with a pat of butter I found in Herbie's fridge. I said goodbye to the guys that night, knowing this was the last time — except for the plane ride home — that I would see them.

Herbie never called me again. I guess I was too much of a wild card to have in his deck.

6

THE GIG FROM HELL

It was a crummy night.

Sheets of water were bombarding our plane while flashes of lightning illuminated the narrow cabin in the sky. The Big Bird bobbed, dipped, and swayed. It was like it was being rocked by a mean spirited, mile high giant with postpartum depression. I was flying in the cradle from hell. The skies were *mucho* "unfriendly." The only thing that kept me cool was the thought that soon, I'd be sitting on my couch with a hot cup of mint tea, watching Rawhide.

I studied the face of the stewardess. She didn't look particularly worried. I decided to take my cue from her. I reclined my seat and checked out an article in *Downbeat* that Potato had given me. It had a couple of lines about him. Potato had dog-eared the complimentary page and underlined the reverential quotation in red ink. "See Yane, I da most skeelful coonga mon in da world."

Of course, it should have said he was the shortest *and* most skillful. He was the only cat whose face was level to mine when we talked. I was 5'2".

When we finally touched down in the Big Apple I split a cab with a couple of the hornplayers that lived midtown. I would be the last one out, since I lived furthest uptown. By the time I reached *my* destination, most of the cab fare would have been paid for by my bandmates.

I silently took in all the neon lights as the cab made its way uptown. I felt soothed and comforted, awash in a sea of fluorescent light particles. It was good to be back in the Big Apple. Being on the road was like taking a vacation with your parents. You had to follow certain rules and stick to rigid time strictures. You were tired or bored most of the time. But — unlike a vacation with your parents — the bandleader still had to pay you, no matter how big a pain in the ass you were.

I yawned, then opened the window to let some fresh air in.

After delivering the horn players to their cribs, I continued uptown. I fought the impulse to close my eyes because I didn't want the cabby to miss my street.

As we pulled up in the front of my building, I noticed my crib looked unusually dark. Not only had a light burnt out in the front hall, but I had a strong suspicion that there wasn't one light on in the pad. I was feeling uneasy as I stuck my key in the door.

Even before I flicked on the light I could tell something was amiss. I could see from the dim light that filtered in the big back window, that the window gates (steel bars in a diamond shaped pattern, that folded in and out like an accordion) were open. They were *always* shut and locked tight.

I flipped on the light. My eyes darted around the room. What was wrong with this picture?

Fuck! Where was my T.V. set? I remembered I had set it up on the window ledge in front of the gates just before I left.

I ran to Renee's room, hoping she had borrowed it.

I opened her door. Unmade bed, clothes strewn all over the floor, half empty bottle of Replique (her favorite perfume) on the dresser. No T.V.

Wishful thinking.

I instinctively started running from room to room, frantically looking for the set. The scene reminded me of the time my uncle Harry got his car stolen. That stupid idiot ran around the block about four times before it sunk in.

Sorry dude, no Chevy in sight ... and no T.V. Who could I call? My mom was two thousand miles away. The police had better things to do. Damn! I wished my roomie was home. Where the hell was Miss Twinkle Toes anyway? And what was the damn window gate doing open?

I hastily unpacked my stuff, unloaded my lace panties in the hamper and threw on some old jeans. Then I sat down on my lumpy couchbed to wait. I was emotionally spent from the gig and the plane ride. I felt like either screaming or crying. I didn't know which.

I put my head in my hands.

Then ...

Clop, clop.

Footsteps in the hall, amplified by the high ceiling and hardwood floor. Two people. Laughter. It was Renee's laugh. But who was the other cat? I listened intently. The voice was deep and husky — familiar. Shit!!! It was Joe's. He was talking about getting a strike or something.

I sat very still as the raucous pair entered. Joe had his arm around Renee. Then he touched her long dark glossy hair. They were three or four paces inside the doorway before they realized they weren't alone.

Renee got the vibe first. As she turned around her mouth flew open. But she instantly regained her composure.

"Oh, I thought you'd be home tomorrow. Joe and me were just out bowling." She sounded so offhanded and breezy. She was employing her phony, gimmie-a-tip, waitress smile.

But I wasn't about to ante up. Not for *that* bitch!

Joe kept his eyes on the floor. It was as if he was trying to decide what kind of reaction was appropriate.

"Where's my fucking T.V.?" I hissed in a kind of controlled rage.

"Oh shit... yeah .... Dog got in here one night. It was so hot last week, I had to open the window. I guess I went out for a few minutes and left the window gate open. Yeah, that's all it took the sonofabitch ...."

I looked at her. She was lying. Renee had been out for longer then a few minutes. I'd lived here for almost two years and nothing — not even a bobbypin — was missing. I put that girl in charge of the fort for a few days and all of a sudden the damn place is under siege And not only property was missing. She'd been hangin' out with the one cat I had my eye on. The *only* cat I.... Bitch!

I was furious! My roomie was a turncoat. My hopes had dissolved — romantic dreams and aspirations dashed against the rocks. *And* I was minus a T.V.

Maybe Joe didn't know how I felt but *she* sure as hell did.

Plus, I was beginning to get the feeling that this had been going on for a long time. All those nights Renee was out having a beer with some cat .... Now I knew *who* the mystery man was. And what about that day I came off the road early when Joe was here and Renee was in her bathrobe? Fuck. This was no new caper — no *new* game they were running on me.

In fact, *this* was the live ammo my roomie had been alluding to.

All of a sudden I didn't want to live in this apartment any more. A spur-of-the-moment decision shaped itself inside my tortured brain.

++++

From the moment I discovered my roomie and my drumsky in romantic cahoots I had started looking for a new crib. I needed a change of habitat.

Everything, all the bright colored pillows on the lumpy couch, the matted prints of Picasso and Rouault hanging on the walls, and the colorful early-American dish, towels in the kitchen, looked dull and dead. I was living in the colorless world of disappointment. Love gone bad. A film *noir*.

Now I was moving to the East Village. I had found a small pad on Avenue A between 2nd and 3rd.

I hadn't spoken to Renee or Joe since that fateful encounter — and I didn't intend to — except for business. That night I had asked Joe for his key, then asked him to leave. Renee had retreated into her bedroom ever since and was now avoiding me like the plague.

She knew the score. Anyway, fuck it! I'd be gone in about three weeks.

The whole episode had left a bad taste in my mouth. I was hurting. I decided, out of self preservation, to start hangin' out again. I really missed being on the scene, the smoky late night jams, the brothers jocularly *talking that trash,* the competition between the players. It was a game of who could play the slickest, fastest, hippest most elongated licks. A game to measure whose fingers were the most like greased lightning. A game I was good at.

For a while I was so obsessed with Joe I had forgotten the reason I'd come to New York.

I no longer had amnesia.

I started making the rounds of the all-night jam sessions going on in some of the midtown and downtown lofts. Soon, I started meeting a lot of different cats, exchanging numbers and getting leads for gigs.

I was coming to life.

One night I walked into Jimmy Braggs' loft and sat in with this great guitar player. His name was Grant Green. He told me he was trying to put a band together for this gig in Indianapolis next week and asked me if I'd be interested. Without hesitation, I said yes.

When I ran his name by a few of the cats, they looked concerned.

"Girl," my friend Carmel Jones said, "if you work with that cat, make sure you get you a nightly draw. I know he's *supposed* to be clean, but there's conflicting stories about him." Carmel shook his neat perfectly shaped dome.

"Shit, man, he aint gonna burn me." I smiled. "He looked clean when I saw him, although he did have a kinda of funny shaped head. Flat in back." I made a straight cut through the air with my hand. "Anyway J. C. Moses and Don Bailey are making the gig. J. C.'s one tough motherfucker. He'll cover my ass."

++++

A week before I moved downtown, I went on the road with Grant, J. C. and Don.

J. C. Moses had a huge yellow Buick from the mid-fifties. The trunk space was so big that he got all his drums inside — plus Grant's amp and guitar. Don's bass fit nicely between the front and back seat. The four of us still had plenty of leg room, even with that big unwieldy hunk of wood between the seats.

Before we got rollin', Grant's old lady stood at the curb, kissed him and gave him quite a lengthy set of instructions. Everything from "take your methadone, and get enough rest," to "don't sleep with any stray bitches." It sounded like Grant needed a baby-sitter.

Grant breathed a sigh of relief as we pulled away from the curb. He smiled and waved to his old lady while at the same time cursing her under his breath.

"That bitch need to stay out of ma bidness," Grant said. Having saved face, he leaned back and lit up a cigarette.

We were off. After we left the outskirts of Manhattan the cats whipped out a joint. So this was how it was going to be.

I opened the window, coughed and waved my hand through the air a couple of times.

We cruised along all afternoon at an easy clip. From the back seat of a big old car — where I usually sat — the most available scenery was the tops of trees. Boring. Our big boat of a car had a faint trail of black smoke coming out of the exhaust pipe when we started up after stopping. J. C. said it was just a cosmetic thing. His short needed a slight adjustment. Which I knew the cat would never get.

We were somewhere in Ohio when things began to get slightly strange. J. C. — who was driving — said he had a feeling the fuzz were following us. The cat was looking real agitated. He said it might be dangerous if the heat saw three black cats in the same vehicle with a white chick.

"Who knows what those assholes are thinkin'. Look baby," J. C. said peering in the rearview mirror at me, "you might get us nailed. Shit they might think we're transportin' something over the state line. Anyway it might not be a bad idea if you got down in your seat a little — especially when we stop for red lights. Wouldn't want those rednecks gettin' the wrong fuckin' idea." J. C. chortled, slurping air between his two missing front teeth.

For the rest of the trip I kind of sat in the corner of the back seat hunched down below window level. Whenever the cats stopped for food — especially at a white establishment — they had me wait in the car lying flat on the seat.

Personally, I thought J. C. was paranoid. But as they say, even if you're paranoid, it doesn't mean they're not out to get you.

By the time we arrived in Indianapolis my back was sore and my neck was stiff.

After a bit, we checked into this funky old three-story hotel in the black section of town. This place was bare bones. A modern box type dwelling with cheap-gold plated door knobs, cheesy steel window frames, and ugly blonde furniture. It had the look and feel of a newly built low-rent apartment building.

Immediately after settling in, the clubowner came over to meet us and see if we were all comfortable.

All I can say is that my skin started to crawl when the cat looked at me. At one point, he patted my back, then started to rub it. I moved away, trying to pretend he didn't really mean anything by his gesture.

After hippin' us to all the cool restaurants in the neighborhood, Mr. Clubowner drove us all to his house to meet his wife. He said she had prepared a meal for us.

When we arrived, his better half, a chubby woman of about sixty, was putting the finishing touches on a hat. In fact, the house was filled with hundreds of hats. She looked me up and down a few times then offered me one of her lids. Since I didn't wear them, I declined. She seemed almost relieved, because her hats were supposedly worth a lot of bread.

After sitting down to a home made meal of chicken-fried steak, cornbread, greens, chitlins, and peach cobbler, we went to the club to drop off the bass, drums and guitar amp and set up the mikes and sound system.

Though the club was fairly large, the bandstand was located in a remote corner of the room under a stairwell. I knew during the soundcheck — this was going to be a bitch of a gig. The sound bounced and boomed in all the wrong places. I could hardly hear the piano and J. C.'s cymbals had a weird kind of washy reverb on them. The guitar sound was completely muted by the walls. Ole Grant sounded like he was literally phoning his part in.

I filed it all away under "more on-the-road bullshit."

When we got back to the hotel there were a couple of ladies waiting for Grant. They were bearing gifts. Being a gracious host, Grant wanted to know if anyone else wanted to get high. I declined. J. C. and Don thought for a second, then decided to take a rain check.

As soon as Grant closed the door to his room, the party began. Since Grant's room was next to mine I heard everything — bursts of laughter, loud voices and little screams of pleasure from Grant and the ladies. These sounds continued for about three hours until everyone (apparently) passed out.

Having eaten earlier that afternoon, I decided to take a little nap. Were these noises going to go on for a full week?

Knock. Knock.

I awoke from my half sleep. J. C. was at the door.

"Anyone hear from Grant?" J. C. had knocked on his door but there was no answer.

I shrugged my shoulders. Then we went next door and knocked again. Still no answer.

"Fuck man, I think Grant's split. We're gonna have to find this place on our own." J. C. said.

I got dressed, then J. C., Don, and I went down to the garage and got into J. C.'s big yellow boat. We then headed for the club, asking directions every couple of miles.

When we got there, Grant was already on the bandstand tuning up. He was looking tired and scratching around the head area. Uh oh. That meant only one thing. Smack. The cat had been riding the "white horse."

After Grant got going, he would play a solo, then start to nod when Don and I played ours. One time Don had to tap Grant on the shoulder to play the head out. By the end of the night we all knew the score.

Before the evening ended, I ran over to the bar to get a draw. This was *de rigueur* when working for a junkie, because you never knew — especially if he was the bandleader — when he would draw everyone's bread for the week.

The bartender, a meticulously neat, thin, grey-haired, light-skinned cat with a towel around his waist, said he had to ask the owner. The bartender came back, stoically keyed open the cash drawer and doled out eighty bucks. J. C. was next to ask for his draw. The bartender again went back to the office. The club owner came out in person.

"I ain't makin' enough dough to give you cats your bread every night, you dig? Ya'll will have ta hold off til' weekend."

"Fuck man, they gonna turn off my lights if I don't send some bread home." J. C. whined.

"Well man," the club owner said tersely, "I'll see what I kin do come tomorrow."

Grant was in the wind almost before the last note was played. J. C. was also starting to get perturbed. Don was trying to smooth down J. C.'s ruffled feathers but it was apparent J. C. was on some kind of collision course with his alter ego.

That night, there were more loud noises from Grant's room. Being in the next room from Grant was kinda like living next door to a combination bodyshop/pigsty. Besides his goings-on being louder than hell, there were plates of half-eaten food on the furniture, balled-up clothes on the floor and dresser, and empty bottles of Jack Daniels strewn about the room. His place was loud and rude.

I fell asleep despite the din.

Next day I knocked on J. C's and Don's door — who were forced to share a room out of financial necessity.

There was some animated conversation, then two women answered.

"Come on in." A tall dark-skinned beauty beckoned. We like ladies too.

I sat on Don's bed for a moment. J. C. had a wild look in his eye. The two of them had been drinking and partying all night, but of course *they* were only doing a little weed.

"Hey baby, watcha know?" Don said.

"What's happenin' with Grant?" I asked. "The cat's been out to lunch since we got here."

"Damn if I know." Don smiled. "His old lady swore he was clean. She don't know the half of it."

"I just wanna get all my bread. One hundred percent. Every last duccet."

"We gonna watch the cat. Don't worry baby!" Don assured me.

With that one of the ladies sat down on the bed next to me and put her arm around my waist. That was my cue to split.

Later that evening Grant disappeared just before the gig again. I surmised that that was the time he scored.

That night the gig was a carbon copy of the previous night. The cat was whacked out of his skull — forehead glistening, head bobbing. From the outside, it looked like Grant was in a softly purring, stress free, pink cloud kind of environment. There was no past, no future and no one to answer to. His universe was a safe dark place with shades drawn.

J. C. drew some bread that night. Unfortunately it was only half of what I drew the night before.

He was hopping mad. Yeah, J. C. — who was a little crazy anyway — was starting to lose it.

++++

It was the anniversary of Malcom X's assassination. I had been up for about an hour when I heard a horrendous ruckus coming from J. C.'s and Don's room. Someone was screaming stomping and pounding on the walls.

I opened my door.

I had a bird's-eye view. Their room was directly across from mine and their door was partially open.

"What the fuck are you doing man?"

"They killed Malcom. Those fuckers killed him. Motha fuckers...."

J. C. was hysterical. Don was trying to calm him down but without much success. Working for a junkie was stressful. You were always in a state of hypervigilance. Because you knew damn well something was gonna go down. Something unexpected, perverse, twisted, and dark.

For a few seconds there was silence. Maybe Don had worked some voodoo. Then I heard the sound of glass breaking. My heart sank.

For a split second I flashed on a Mormon girl I had known in high school. Marva was pretty, blond, and wore pigtails. She was probably happily married now with a nice husband, a normal life and a cute little tract house. If only I ....

I was jerked out of my reverie. The violence escalated.

J. C. had started to throw the furniture out of the window. He was ranting and sobbing in a kind of hoarse voice a kid has when his little tantrum goes unchecked. J. C. had succeeded in trashing one lamp and an end table on the sidewalk below. Now he was trying to stuff a chair through the window. But he was defied by the law of physics, the chair being too big.

I was watching from my door frame as two burly guys from building maintenance ran down the hall to subdue the cat. Don escorted the two guys into the room as I looked on in horror. After a brief tussle the goons grabbed J. C. by the shoulders, flung him around and pinned him to the ground. Then one of them punched him in the nose. I could hear a squishing sound as the bones broke. The other guy followed suit as he blackened one of J. C.'s eyes and punched him in the stomach. After the cat lay prostrate for a few minutes they took him to the hospital.

Grant, hearing the ruckus taking place, ambled out of his room to investigate. He was in an dirty undershirt. I could see fresh track marks on his arms. He looked like death warmed over. The cat had a ghostlike almost negative glow around him, like he was being illumined by a light from the underworld. Standing right behind him was the same chick he'd had in his room the other day. But she didn't look foxy anymore. There were horrible black circles under her eyes and bruises all over her body.

After the cats hauled J. C. to the hospital, Grant — without a word — stumbled back into his den of iniquity.

I went to sit down on my bed. I was shaking. Too much stimuli. If this gig were a style of music, it would've been a combination of the low down dirty blues and Stravinsky's *Rites of Spring.*

To clear my mind, I caught a bus downtown and walked in and out of a few shops. I sighted a Woolworth's in a little enclave of stores and browsed for a while. Then I found the knitting section. For the next hour and a half I picked up and examined different-colored spools of yarn. Finally after focusing on a pale lavender skein and running my hands over the soft wool, I went back to the hotel.

By the time I had returned, J. C. was back from the hospital. His nose was all bandaged and there was salve around his eyes. Don was trying to be affable but J. C. was sullen.

The three of us rode to the gig in silence.

When we arrived, Grant was stoned again. Nothing was said about J. C.'s little brush with insanity.

We played the same old bebop tunes; "Confirmation," Au Privave," " Night in Tunisia," " Woody'n You" etc. Despite the day's happenings we got a little finger tappin' groove going. But on this gig, every night was a rerun. Grant played some great lines, but he generally followed them with cliches. I guess he didn't want to leave his musical safety zone since every other aspect of his life was like a high wire act without a net.

Personally, I was glad this gig was almost over. Just one more night to go.

I only wanted the music to be explosive. Not the situation.

++++

The last day of the gig I got up and went to check on J. C. He seemed almost normal. Maybe heaving furniture *was* a good release. He and Don were drinking a brewsky and playing dominoes.

"Hey guys, what time are we leaving tomorrow?" I asked J. C., as he owned and operated the old jalopy we were driving.

"Oh, ah... about ten a.m." J. C. said, moving one of the rectangular black pieces with several white dots on it. "I figure if we can be on the road by ten, we'll hit New York in the 'wee small,' baby."

"Anyone tell Grant?"

"No, we'll hip him to it at the gig tonight." J. C. moved another tile.

"Don, you been gettin' any draws, man?"

"Uh uh. I thought I'd get my bread all in one chunk. If I buy too much shit, my ol' lady complains."

"Damn, I need all the bread I can get. I'm movin' when I get back to town and that ain't cheap."

I watched the cats move the little black rectangles around for a few minutes, then I went to my room and turned on the T.V. Being on the road was boring, but this gig fluctuated between being boring and dangerously exciting.

Later that night we informed Grant that we were leaving about ten.

Grant smiled, shaking his flat head up and down, and profusely thanking us all for working with him. "Just knock on my door when y'all are ready. I'll be all shined, shitted, and shaved," he volunteered.

++++

Next morning very early, there was a knock on my door. I roused myself from some stupid dream and stumbled to the door. It was Mr. Clubowner.

"Hey Miss Getz." The old dude looked like he had something on his mind. "Wanna make fifty extra bucks? Only take a few minutes of your time."

All of a sudden my antenna was up. *Red Alert!* The cat wanted me to turn a trick.

"Sorry man, I'm not into it."

"You inta ladies or somethin'?"

At that point I just, looked at him, smiled and shrugged my shoulders. "Ya never know." I said with a wink. I figured the less outraged I seemed by his offer, the better. No big deal.

He stood there for a second then turned around and left. Uh uh, I wasn't about to challenge a 250 pound guerilla to a wrestling match. Not in the A.M. anyway!

I went back to sleep for a few hours, then got up and had breakfast.

I knocked on J. C. and Don's door at the crack of ten. They were all packed and ready to go. We were all anxious to get back to our own "on top of the beat," edgy, avant garde, hip little worlds. Now all we had to do was collect Grant, get our bread and pay our hotel bill.

"Man, go knock on Grants door." J. C. said. "See if the dude's ready. We gotta be in the wind soon 'cause I got a gig tomorrow night."

I went to Grant's door and put my knuckles to the wood.

Knock, knock, motherfucker.

No answer. I knocked a little harder. Nothin'.

After a few more attempts I went back to J. C.'s and Don's room.

"No one answers. The cat's either stoned or dead. Maybe you wanna go over and try?"

J. C. strode out of the room. He stood outside Grant's room and pounded on the door.

"Fuck, I'm goin' downstairs and get the pass key. That motherfucker's either so stoned or...."

J. C. ran to the stairs and vaulted down. A second later he was back, accompanied by a cat from the front desk.

The clerk stuck the key in the door.

J. C. and I walked in. The room looked empty.

I ran to the closets while J. C. hurriedly opened and closed all the drawers.

The cat had checked out in the middle of the night. There was nothing there. Not one stitch of clothing, not one matchbook. No sign anyone had inhabited the room in the past few days. The cat had made a clean getaway.

For the second time, J. C. freaked. This time he had a reason.

Ol' Grant Green had absconded with all our funds. *Our fucking bread.* Except for our little cash draws, we had all worked this whole week for nothin'. Zip. Goose egg.

++++

J. C. drove like a bat out of hell. The few bucks that I had had the foresight to draw, all went into the gas tank. Yeah, his short was a guzzler.

The whole trip, J. C. fantasized about killing Grant — choking him, hitting him upside the head, wringing his neck. At one point J. C. was even contemplating the possibility of slitting Grant's throat.

"Yeah, but he's not a singer man." I said. "What point would there be in taking his pipes out?" I flashed on all the lame singers with sequined tops. How many times could one idiot sing "More?"

"I dig," J. C. said laughing. "Anyway what goes around, comes around, don't it!"

"Shit yeah," I said. "Anyway I know some cats at the union. I'm gonna go rap with them."

"Dream on baby cakes." Don had suddenly awakened from his nap. Those cat's take your bread and make nicey nicey, but they don't *do* shit!"

Before I could answer him, he was in the prone position again.

I don't know how fast J. C. was driving, but we were back in the Big Apple in record time.

When I got back to the crib, it was empty. Renee had left a note saying she was visiting her parents in Baltimore for a week. Actually I had almost forgiven her. But I was glad to be alone for a while. As for Joe, I had no interest in him anymore. I didn't even know why. Shit, how could you moon over, obsess, give over your whole being to someone and then — in the blink of an eye — lose interest? Well maybe if the fascination had been mutual ....

++++

Local 802 was always buzzing. People were scurrying back and forth like little beavers and mostly accomplishing nothing.

Today *somebody* was going to help me. I was determined.

I showed my union card then asked to see a representative. The clerk pointed me to a chair and told me I could see the next available cat.

About a half an hour later, the clerk directed me to another office, where I was told someone would see me shortly.

I was sitting there for forty five minutes when some old guy with a bad rug came out of his office and told me I was in the wrong department.

I was spirited to another section, where yet someone else assured me someone would hear my complaint *very soon.*

Very soon, turned into another hour.

Then a bolt of red hot anger hit me. Perhaps it was the culmination of all the adverse bullshit I had gone through in the prior week but some unholy spirit swept over me. I got up from the chair and screamed.

"I want to see the president of this fucking union. Send the president. I pay my fucking dues. I *want* to see the president!!"

Two or three representatives came running out of their offices. Everyone was trying to calm me down, but I was on a roll. The more I screamed, the stronger I got. A crowd of people had gathered around me.

Suddenly the Red Sea parted. The group stepped out of the way. An old man with a combover, a green v-neck cardigan, and pristine white shoes, emerged from the shadows.

My hero on a white horse had arrived.

"What do you want, dolly? Whatsa matter? I'm Max, the President. Come on into my office sweetheart, let's see what we can do for you."

I followed Max into his office as the crowd disbanded.

"What's the problem dahling? Maybe we can do a little something for you."

Who *was* this guy, the Wizard of Oz?

I told the sweet old man about the trip with Grant and how he had burned all of us. Max lit a cigar and leaned back in his cracked leather chair. I also tearfully told him about how I was counting on the money from that gig, to move downtown.

The old man looked sympathetically at me, then spoke.

"Listen, dolly. We can't do much about this here, because I'm almost positive Mr. Green didn't send in a contract. And even if he did, we're not the police, we're just the Union. We don't track down musical felons." The old guy paused for a moment then looked up. "But I tell you what I'm gonna do personally. How much was Mr. Green gonna pay you?"

"Three hundred dollars."

Max reached into his pocket and pulled out a roll of bills. He took three crisp new one hundred dollar bills off the top and handed them to me.

"Okay dolly. *I'm* gonna give you the three hundred bucks. But in return I want you to play for my grandson's Bar Mitzvah. Be at the Sheraton Hotel in Queens 3:30 sharp, next Saturday. Do we have a deal?"

"Yep!" I beamed. "Thanks Max!!"

++++

That Saturday, I played for Max's grandson's Bar Mitzvah. The following week I moved downtown.

As far as I was concerned, Grant Green was history!

7

SEIZURE

It was a great day for moving. Just a hint of autumn in the air and a cloudless sky. I was just shoving some odds and ends in some boxes, when I heard the sound of hubcaps scraping up against the curb. The moving truck was here.

My traitorous roomie was at work, so I didn't have to conspicuously snub her or pretend I was above it all and say goodbye.

I hoped she and Joe would be happy. But Joe was too involved in his own shit to care about someone else's. I was too. Playing good took *lots* of practice time. Right now I was practicing sequences of fourth chords and notating Coltrane solos. "Blowin' your ass off," took a concerted effort. Yeah, and moving took up too damn much time.

I rushed into the kitchen to see if I had packed my coffee pot.

Knock. Knock.

"Midtown Movers."

Midtown Movers were supposed to be the best and the cheapest. They came highly recommended by Jerome Richardson, who knew everyone and everything.

As I opened the door, a huge burly dude stuck his big meaty paw out. "Hey lady, my name's Sal." I heartily pumped his hand a few times, then gave it back.

"Tell me exactly what's gonna go in da truck."

I pointed to a corner of the living room where I had sequestered a chest of drawers, a lumpy couch, a huge stack of clothes, and a newly purchased grand piano.

Well, it looked like a grand piano, but as I soon found out — looks weren't everything. The fucking thing was worthless. Some old lady had sold it to me dirt cheap. I'd mistakenly thought I'd have a piano tuner come and fix it, but as I soon found out, you just couldn't repair a piece of junk. The sounding board was cracked and some of the hammers were misfiring and needed replacing. But of course there were no parts available because it was an *el cheapo* model from the thirties. A "show" type piano folks put in their living rooms but never played. Well at least it was a Chickering — my grandma had one of those. Maybe I'd find a sucker and resell it.

Fortunately, Sal said the thing was lightweight and easily movable. Sal quickly briefed his "boys" on what was going where, then proceeded to. load up the truck. After that, we set out for the Lower East side. An easy twenty minutes in real time, but conceptually, a world away.

Sal was ahead of schedule and in a good mood, so he obligingly let me ride in the front seat. He had one of those white paneled jobs with cracked brown leather upholstery and no shocks. It was fun riding up high, and looking down at traffic from a bouncing, swerving, continuously honking, truck.

I felt happy as we rode toward lower Manhattan. It was good to be in a big noisy bustling metropolis, making my own way and making a few waves to boot. I was young and hopeful. My new crib was in the neighborhood where all the young happening cats hung. Soon, I'd be right in the middle of all the *cool* shit.

By mid afternoon I was all moved in. The only hitch had been getting the piano up the stairs. One of Sal's helpers had chipped a small piece off the white marble stairs, but who would know?

I sat down to take a breather, surveying my digs. The rooms were postage-stamp size, smaller than my 91st. St crib. The grand piano took up most of the living room, so I had to put my couch in the kitchen/bedroom. After trying a few maneuvers, I put my chest of drawers near the front door. They made a good room divider. The crib was cramped, but cozy.

The walls were another matter. My crib had been previously occupied by a couple of hippies who'd painted pink and blue clouds on the walls. Some of that hippie stuff (rainbows, clouds, trees and flowers on the walls) reminded me of kindergarten.

I was too old for *that* now.

++++

The next day was spent painting. Soon the walls were a nice boring utilitarian white. I picked up the phone. Maybe someone would meet me at Slugs later. Jackie McLean was jammin' that night.

No go. Marvin and George were busy.

I went solo.

Upon arrival, I showed my fake I. D., and looked for a strategic place to sit.

Slugs was a typical Lower Eastside jazz hang. Sawdust floors, old wooden tables, and "jazz art" on the walls. Art that looked like it was painted by some six year old schizoid who had forgotten his medication. Why did jazz art always look like the artist never cleaned his brushes?

I'd once asked some "jazz artists" *what* had inspired them? Most of them told me that they simply painted to the sounds of the great ones: Miles, Trane, Bud and Bird.

Admittedly, they had no technical training, but the sheer power of the music kind of swept them up, carried them away, and guided their hands.

By *that* rationale, I could just put on an inspiring L.P. and instantly design a city or whip an awesome collection of designer clothes. Yeah, just throw that record on the turntable and *voila.*

But bad art wasn't the only constant in Lower Eastside jazz clubs. Smoke hung in the air like some carcinogenic fog. And there was that familiar, cheesy, old-socks, pizza smell, infused with a pungent stale beer and wine odor. A smell you hated at first, then warmed up to. An "acquired smell."

Finding a table could be difficult too, because the lighting was bad and lots of people table-hopped so you never knew *who* was sitting *where.* But I was fortunate. After checking out the scene for a minute, I spotted a little table near the bandstand. Seating myself, I looked up from my little niche and nodded to Larry Ridley, who was up on the bandstand, tuning up his bass. I had met him on some hotel gig in Brooklyn. Larry returned my nod, then leaned over and whispered something to Jackie who subsequently turned around and looked at me.

Midway through the second set, Jackie asked me to sit in. As I walked up to the bandstand, I took in the vibe. Damn! Being a part of a jazz group was like being an angel in some hip kind of heaven. You were one of the ordained, one of the musically blessed, that caught snatches of melodies running through the ether and brought them down to earth. Horace Silver had gotten it right when he named his group the Jazz Messengers.

Before I left, Jackie asked me if I could sub for John Hicks on Friday.

I was in the thick of things now. So what, if the lower East Side was a hot bed of junkies. I would just be extra careful, that's all.

At the end of the night, I even had one of the cats I knew stand in the street with me while I got a cab. The lower East Side between Avenue C and D was no place to hang. That is, unless, you wanted to score.

++++

In a matter of weeks I was getting all kinds of "downtown gigs." Maybe my roommate had done me a favor.

My friend Marvin called one night and said Freddie Hubbard was playing at Slugs. "Baby, I'll just swing by and pick you up. Freddie'll probably ask you to blow. Be ready!"

When we got there the place was packed. There was a lot of friction in the air. Freddie was known as a bad boy, so people came to hear him play and see if he was going to act up. His behavior was a kind of residual entertainment.

Playing with Freddie, was Larry Ridley on bass. James Spaulding on alto, Clifford Jarvis on drums and Cedar Walton on piano. It was a heavy lineup.

Though Marvin and I were sitting near the back, Spalding caught sight of me pointed me out to Freddie. Freddie pretended to ignore me, then a few tunes later, he asked me to come up and play. As I slid over the piano bench, Freddie put my ass to the fire. He called "Cherokee."

It was one of those tunes the Big Dogs tested the younger cats with. A chop tester. Fast and furious with a million changes.

Freddie not only played it rapidly, he played it in the key of B (an unorthodox key for that song). But unbeknownst to Freddie, I had been practicing it for months in B.

I had the two-bat theory of practice. If you make it incredibly hard on yourself, how could *anyone* possibly throw you a curve. At one point in my life I had even practiced with wool gloves on.

I was ready for Freddie.

He was impressed. Although Freddie didn't say anything, he asked me to play a few more tunes. A good indication, because at that time in New York, if a cat didn't dig you, you were given the boot. Instantly removed. Forcibly ejected. Baby, you were gone! See ya!

A few days later Freddie called me. Cedar couldn't make all the nights at Slugs. Would I be interested?

++++

I practiced a few extra hours every day in anticipation of Freddie's gig. I wanted to kick ass. I also had aspirations of hanging with the A list type cats — Freddie's crowd.

The first night of the gig, I was really nervous. To make matters worse I was almost late, because it was hard to get a cab to go down to Ave. C or D.

I got there without a second to spare, raced in the door and ran up to the bandstand. Spaulding smiled and nodded, but Freddie ignored me and counted off the first tune. It was some medium tempo standard that I wasn't that familiar with. It was an easy tune, so I caught on quickly. But as the night went on, Freddie just played what he wanted to play without any regard as to whether *I* knew the song or not. He just stared straight ahead with his cold dark eyes and did what he damn pleased. Tunes I didn't know, I had to learn on the spot. It was sink or swim.

For the more intricate stuff, Spaulding would run over to the piano with a leadsheet or a piece of paper with chords he had jotted down. Ol' Freddie acted like it was none of his concern.

Later in the evening, Freddie took me aside.

"Hey man, ya *gotta* get here a little earlier tomorrow. I got some tunes I wanna show you."

"Sure man. I tried to tonight but..."

Freddie walked away. No excuses. He had better things to do — like hit on some fox at the bar.

++++

I arrived early the next night. A few of the cats in the band were there, but Freddie hadn't shown yet.

It was time to time to hit — still no Freddie, so we started without him.

Halfway through the set, Freddie rushed in cursing under his breath. Something about his old lady.

He called "Without a Song," so fast, my fingers felt like they were going to fall off. Tonight, Freddie, aside from being, aloof and standoffish, was agitated. I pretended that I didn't notice.

During the break, Freddie walked over to me with a couple of leadsheets.

"Here, man, I just wrote these." He said, putting two scribbly pieces of manuscript paper on the piano. "I'm recording next week, and I'm all jammed up trying to come up with some tunes."

I nodded. Then I had a thought.

"Freddie, I've been doin' a little writing these past few months. Maybe, if you have some free time, you could check some of my tunes out. It'd be *so* groovy if you recorded something of mine. Yeah man, I'd be honored."

Freddie looked up from the leadsheet like something had just occurred to him. For a second he connected.

"Hey listen ... why don't I come over to your crib after the gig. I'm. goin' uptown anyway. That cool?"

Wow. This was so easy. Maybe I'd actually made a breakthrough. It felt like I'd just lobbed the ball out of the park. Who knows? Now Freddie was talking to me. If I was *really* lucky, he might use one of my tunes.

++++

After the gig, Freddie flagged down a cab and we set out for my crib.

"Freddie man, don't mind the mess. I'm still getting settled. I just moved a few months ago."

"Yeah. Weren't you Uptown for a minute?"

"Yeah. My crib was under Jerome Richardson's. But I wanted to be where all the *real* shit was happenin'."

"Well, baby, you're in the pocket now."

The cab stopped and I opened my purse. Before I could get out some bread, Freddie pulled a wad of bills from his back pocket.

"I got it!"

"Hey thanks, man."

Freddie nodded and we walked upstairs.

The crib was in total chaos. I had tried on at least ten outfits before the gig. They were all in a random pile on my lumpy couch. As Freddie walked in, I threw the clutter on the floor.

The sink was littered with dishes and tubes of paints. I had been doing pen-and-ink, line drawings then infusing them with a kind of washy color. It was an interesting experiment. No one had seen them yet. I was thinking of showing a few to Freddie.

"Want any tea or coffee?" Like a good hostess I was hoping to make Freddie relaxed and comfortable.

"Have anything cold, baby?"

"Just some Fresca. That cool?"

"Yeah. Sure."

I poured Freddie a glass of the fizzy grape-fruity drink and watched him sneeze. It was funny. Sometimes the carbonation would go up your nose.

I watched Freddie take a few more sips. He was pretty frenetic, like a high-strung thoroughbred. I wanted to cool him out so he could concentrate on the tunes I had written.

Then I had a brainstorm. One of my friends had given me a joint a few days ago. Maybe ....

"Hey man. I got some dynamite weed."

Freddie's face lit up. "'Shit, fire that sucker up and give me a hit."

I opened my little canister with the Christmas scene on it. *Over the river and through the woods ... Yeah,* but me and Freddie weren't going to grandma's house.

I lit the J, took a hit, then passed it to Freddie.

"I usually don't smoke but one of the cats brought it over."

Freddie was already in the ozone when I brought out some of my pen-and ink-stuff.

I've never showed these to anyone but ...."

Freddie grabbed the drawings out of my hand. For a few minutes he was lost in all the lines and squiggles. He turned the paper upside down, on it's side, then held it at arm's length and squinted.

Then he picked the joint up from the ashtray and fired it up again. Instead of offering me another hit, he just held it and smoked it. His eyes were starting to look glazed.

I wandered over to the piano in the living room. Even in the living room I was only a. few feet away from Freddie, the place being so small.

I opened the creaky old piano bench and got out a few tunes I had just penned. Now was the perfect time for me to hit Freddie with them. The cat was cooled out — defenses down.

As I started to play, Freddie called to me.

"Hey, baby, c'mere. Got somethin' I wanna show you."

I stopped playing. What the hell did he want?

Annoyed, I got up and walked a few feet into the kitchen/bedroom.

I stood there a few seconds as Freddie looked at me.

"No baby, closer."

I tentatively took a step toward Freddie.

Freddie pointed to his crotch. "It's getting bigger. Yeah, now it's really huge. Don't you wanna see it?"

I instinctively took a step backwards.

Fuck. In the space of a few seconds things had gotten nasty. What was that sonovabitch up to. *This* was like a cartoon. One where a happy, carefree little duck walks down a garden path and a giant boulder inexplicably appears and mysteriously lands on his head. It was that "out of nowhere" kind of shit.

Before I could say a word Freddie leaned over and grabbed my arm.

Now Freddie Hubbard was a big cat. He held tightly to my arm while he unzipped his pants.

"No, man. Fucking stop it." I screamed. "I don't want to see it!"

"You know you do. *All* you bitches do. Man, chicks love it. C'mere, I want you to do something for me."

Frantically I tried to wriggle away. But his hand tightened on my arm. I started to struggle. Everything in the room was getting brighter. I couldn't breathe. The harder I struggled, the tighter he gripped — like one of those woven, straw Mexican finger vices. A few seconds later, he had secured both my arms.

I felt like I was drowning.

What to do? .... Shit! I started to scream even louder. And then I did something that was totally instinctual.

I started to shake all over like I was having a seizure. Once I started doing it my whole body fell into line, shaking, vibrating twitching, ticking, jerking, and spazzing out. It was like I was motorized. My head started to twist and bob, my teeth started to chatter. Everything was fluttering, modulating, twirling, spasming in perfect synchronicity.

I looked like a windup toy on acid.

Freddie let go of my arms. His eyes got wider. He looked terrified. Then he started to shake his head and back away. "What the fuck's happenin? Shit! I ...I ... I ... gotta split."

With that Freddie Hubbard turned tail and ran out the front door.

++++

It was hard to stop shaking after he left. Once you set something like that in motion, it has to slow down of it's own accord. Even if you're faking it, there's still a physical component.

After unwinding, I called Henry Grimes, who lived about a block away. We'd been friends since I came to New York.

I was upset, but I didn't realize the extent of the trauma I had just been through until I started to talk.

"Man that cat fucking tried to rape me!" Now I was sobbing hysterically. "Mother-fucker!!!"

I looked down. I hadn't noticed all the scratches and bruises until now. I was covered everywhere with smarting red welts, bloody scratches, and more than a few big ugly black and blue marks on my arms where Freddie had tried to forcibly hold me.

I heard Henry curse. I could picture him shaking his head.

"Hold tight. I'll be over in a second."

Henry hastily put down the receiver. About three minutes later he was at my door. He had brought a duffel bag over with some supplies. He had bandages, antiseptic plus an old German Luger from World War II.

Henry hastily unzipped his bag and started to swab my wounds with cotton and stingy stuff. His eyebrows were knit together as if he were trying to concentrate and control his emotions.

After attending to my wounds, Henry retrieved something else from the bottom of the bag.

"What ja gonna do with *that?*" I asked Henry as he took out the piece.

"I'm gonna kill that bastard, that's what. All I need is some bullets."

I could see it now. The Jazz Trial of the century. Henry Grimes wasting away in the big house for poppin' Freddie Hubbard.

In the course of the trial, the whole story would come out and...soon I'd be the most hated person in jazz. Not that fucking idiot, Freddie. *Me.* The cats would think I flaunted myself in front of Freddie and when the shit came down, I wouldn't put out. I'd be the chick with the apple. The destroyer. The *persona non grata.* No one would call me for gigs anymore. I'd be one forgotten, despised, out of work, side man.

Oh God, what if I had to get a day gig?

"Whoa, Henry, man. Hold it. I think we better think this over carefully," I said, still shaking. "Look, I wouldn't shed too many tears if I heard the cat got beaten up, but offing him? Damn! That sounds like a bad move. Nix. Ah, uh. Cancel. I mean like who would Sonny Rollins use on bass if you were in the joint?"

Henry stopped dead in his tracks. He loved playing with Sonny.

"Well man, then I'll just have to beat him within an inch of his life."

++++

In about a week I felt a little calmer. Henry couldn't find Freddie, so he soon forgot about pounding him.

But something had happened to me that night, that I can't explain. Freddie had taken the wind out of my sails. I was more cautious. More reticent. When I thought of the future I no longer envisioned an endless montage of sunny days. Now there was something lurking.

Something wasn't right.

Before I came to New York, I'd always pictured Big Dogs as idealistic musical revolutionaries. People who *lived* for the musical cause. Straight ahead, relentless practitioners of bebop who put nothing above their art. Now, the great artist myth was starting to erode.

I still loved to play, write, hang with the cats and soak up the New York vibe. But there was something beneath surface working it's way up.

++++

After the encounter with Freddie, I never let anyone into my crib, unless I really knew them. I wasn't quite so eager to be accommodating. And for the first time I figured if I wasn't accepted in the world of jazz, there were other worlds out there.

Strangely, I never saw Freddie after that night. Though I had many gigs in lots of different venues I never as much as glimpsed the cat again. Even from a distance.

Which was just fine.

8

STAN-NO
RELATION-GETZ

I'd had it. Living on the Lower East Side was a drag. Ever since my encounter with Freddie Hubbard, things had turned sour. The once charming little storefronts, run by Russian immigrants, rich hippies, soapbox revolutionaries, and barefoot Gypsies were getting old. The garbage on the streets, junkies blocking your way at every turn, the smell of pot in the air and the old crones dressed in all black, clicking their teeth and vociferously rapping their canes on the sidewalk, were starting to bug me.

I'd been to the Village a number of times and I always enjoyed walking around the area. There were the quaint little two-and three-story buildings with trees in front of them,

---

flower pots in the windows and successful arty-type people strolling around in hip bright threads. Things seemed less uptight. The rents were a little higher, but I was sure there were some good deals to be had.

Then there were the numerous coffee houses where, on any given day, cool in-the-know kind of people were discussing, ruminating and solving life's great riddles while munching organic muffins, drinking espresso, and smoking Gaulois'.

This was where I wanted to move.

Besides, my present landlord had accused me of chipping a piece of the hall stairwell leading to my apartment. One morning I found a bill for over a hundred bucks in my mailbox.

Damn, I thought the building was deserted when I'd moved in.

Who was watching?

Perhaps the walls had eyes *and* ears. Anyway, Mr Landau, my creepy little landlord, was getting nothing from me. Zip. I told him to sue Midtown Movers, but he informed me that they were no longer in business. Well was that *my* fault?

Yeah, there were all kinds of signs, telling me to split.

Miraculously, after searching for less then a week, I found a one-bedroom pad on Christopher Street, near Sixth, for $93 bucks a month. A choice second floor apartment in a locked building with an elevator. I chucked it up to Divine providence since everyone told me there were no places in the Village for under two hundred a month.

I gave the landlady a deposit, painted the new place a purplish white, packed up all my junk, hired another moving truck, and moved in. In a matter of days I was set up, ready to go.

My new crib had a real kitchen (small though it was), a real bathroom with a combination tub/shower, a bedroom, and a living room. I now had a place that my friends would envy.

I promised myself I would never, ever move again. I decided if I had to suddenly leave the country, or go back to California, I would sublet. *Who* in their right mind would give up a rent-controlled apartment in world-famous Greenwich Village?

The scene was picture perfect, except for one thing. At least three or four times a week, I heard a loud thudding sound coming from my upstairs neighbor's apartment. Sometimes it continued for as long as fifteen minutes. I finally concluded (after much speculation), that the couple above me were practicing bowling. *Maybe* they were even in a league.

I had seen them a few times in the elevator. They were a typical sixties' couple. He was a black, tightly muscled, good looking guy with hooded eyes and a bit of a swagger. She was a petite little redhead with freckles, who wore granny dresses and wire rimmed glasses. They looked like they'd been on a few acid trips and were now "in the flo." They seemed happy enough. Or maybe they were just smilers, folks whose mouths perpetually turned up at the corners.

The only time their noise really bothered me was when I was trying to meditate. But live and let live was my philosophy. What if *I* wanted to make some noise?

The thing on my mind now was work. I was running out of bread. I needed a cash infusion.

I called Chick Corea. He said something was brewing and to expect a call from him in about a day or so. I had heard he was working with Stan Getz, but maybe something even bigger was on the horizon for *him*. Fine. I'd take the leftovers.

I started thinking about working with Stan. But what if Chick had something else in mind? I decided not to jump the gun. Exploring my new neighborhood, seemed like more fun than sitting in the living room, speculating.

++++

I was in the kitchen when the phone rang. I ran out of the little cubicle, my hands full of cookie dough and picked up the receiver. I just knew it was Chick.

"Yeah" I answered, trying not to get the phone all doughy.

"Jane — Stan Getz here. Chick gave me your number."

Stan spoke in a perfect monotone. He sounded like he was reading from the phone book.

"I've got a gig in North Carolina next week. What's your schedule?"

"Ah .... well, I'm working next weekend," I lied, "but I can get out of it." Who wants to waltz with a chick who's got an empty dance card? I was just giving myself some leverage.

"Cool. We're meeting at La Guardia, 5:00 P.M. Sunday. See you there." Stan hung up. The cat never modulated his voice once during the whole conversation.

New York, New York!! One minute you're twiddling your thumbs, the next, you're running with some Big Dog pulling down that long bread.

++++

A week later I was en route to Raleigh. As I boarded the plane I spotted Stan, recognizing him from his pictures. Sitting in back of Stan was Jack DeJohnette and Miroslav Vitous. This was a heavy lineup.

I walked over to the empty seat waiting for me next to Jack.

As I sat down, Stan looked up and greeted me. He was cordial, but distant and a little withdrawn. Jack was different. I could tell by his demeanor that he didn't have a mean bone in his body. Miroslav was another story. He was young and arrogant. Bass players were another breed. They were kind of like the finicky cats of jazz. High strung and temperamental.

And like their feline counterparts, they sometimes needed to be declawed.

During the plane ride, I bonded with Jack. He was interested in the same rock bands that I was. We made a date to catch some concerts when we got back to New York.

I was starting to feel comfortable.

After the plane landed, some lady picked Stan up, while the clubowner drove the three of us to a small motel next door to the club. Nothing fancy but it would do.

The only odd thing so far was that Stan never once mentioned the music. As we were checking in, I asked Jack what kind of stuff Stan was into.

"Oh, Stan plays the same tunes he's recorded. "Desafinado," "How Insensitive" — you know...Jobim. Easy, you won't have any problem."

I had known some Brazilian cats when I was playing with Herbie. That kind of stuff had a different feel to it. But how hard could the Bossa Nova be?

I spent the next day visiting with my friend Daphne — a recent expatriate from New York. She had — in less than six months — single-handedly built a cabin in the woods of Raleigh.

I was very impressed as I surveyed her handiwork. I couldn't stop complimenting her on her herb garden, hand crafted furniture, water pump, and electrical generator.

Although she likened her plot of land to Eden, she was missing one of the perks that Eve had — namely Adam. Who the hell would want to live in the wilderness alone? Too much heavy lifting, as far as I was concerned.

For several hours, we walked in the woods, ate organic home grown vegetables and talked about leading a spiritual life. Then it was back to reality.

Thankfully so, for me.

Nature-girl drove me back to the hotel in her old army jeep. I asked her if she wanted to stay and check out the music, but Daphne shook her head.

"Sorry darlin'. Smoky clubs and boozed-up people don't do it for me. I like the solitude of the forest. Nighttime in the woods is about as noisy as I like it. You ought to spend a night in the cabin sometimes — get your head clear."

"Thanks, Daphne. I'll call you."

Oh yeah. Daphne still had a phone.

I ran upstairs to my room and put on my gig attire. I now had collected about five outfits, all the way from casual to formal. The requirements for good gig outfits were: no body parts showing (so as not to distract people, especially the other players), no light colors (they'd always be at the cleaners), no tight sleeves or armholes (I needed a full range of motion), and no fussy or feminine stuff (I wanted to blend in with the band).

I had decided to wear one of my no nonsense black suits for the first night of the gig. As I checked myself out in the mirror I thought the outfit looked too severe. I impulsively clasped a simple black velvet choker around my neck, then scampered out the door and ran across the motel lawn to the club.

As I entered the smoky establishment, Stan casually looked in my direction. Then he squinted and did a double take. Maybe he expected me to wear a dress or show a little skin. Who knows. Whatever the case, I'd been alone at the bar for about five minutes, when Stan walked up to me. As he came closer, I noticed he was all sweaty, like he had doused his head with water.

He grabbed a napkin from the bar to mop his face.

"Just lost about twenty five pounds," he bragged.

Damn! Beside opening with a non-sequitur, the cat hadn't even said hello.

"I did it on a diet of baked potatoes — spuds with nothing on them. All ya have to do is sprinkle a little vinegar on and ...." Stan made a kissing sound with his mouth while at the same time bunching the tips of his fingers together and opening them up. I had seen a few French chefs do that motion.

"You look groovy — real svelte," I said. Not knowing what he looked like when he was twenty five pounds heavier, I felt obligated to say *something*.

"That's a nice suit," Stan volunteered. "Know how to keep the crease in your pants sharp?"

I shook my head.

"You take them and line them up by the cuffs and hang them upside down in the bathroom when you're taking a shower. Steam works beautifully. Saves a lot on your cleaning bills!" Stan said knowingly.

Just as I was about to thank him for the grooming tip, he spotted a woman in the audience.

"We hit in five. Jack will tell you the lineup." Stan scurried off.

Jack knew the book perfectly. I guess they played the same tunes in the same order every night. Stan didn't want to waste any time organizing a new set.

The first set started out with Bossa Novas.

Halfway through the second tune, Stan turned around and told me I was too busy. I was playing too much shit — attacking the tunes like I was blowing with John Coltrane or Wayne Shorter. The sound was much more casual — breezy.

This stuff was mellow-roony. I had to take a different tact. Like imagining I was lying on the beach in Rio as I was playing. Maybe after I'd learned the book, I could phone my part in.

Though I sounded better on the second set, I still didn't have the right feel. To make matters worse, Miraslav had started making snide comments about my musical ability.

Meow, baby. Sticks and stones ....

Although I wasn't quite up to snuff on my part yet, I was blown away by Stan's ability to turn a phrase. The cat was so melodic. Sometimes when you thought you knew where he was going, he'd take you in an entirely different direction.

Stan was a certified Big Dog.

++++

Once I got into the flavor of the music, the week went by quickly. I was really starting to groove with all the Brazilian rhythms. I also had gotten to know a little about Stan. I say a little, because he was one of those cats that was virtually unknowable. Although he wore his emotions on his sleeve, you had no idea what his thought processes were. How did he get from A to B? Or did he?

What motivated the guy?

I knew he was married, but I couldn't help but notice that he went off with a different lady every night. Of course, a lot of musicians indulged themselves sexually, but Stan was way beyond a little fling now and then.

On the last night of the gig, Stan's mind was wandering. He was distracted. He had exhausted the supply of available ladies in the audience by either hitting on them or going home with them. The cat was looking increasingly frustrated as he cast about for one last amorous adventure in Raleigh.

Then something strange happened. I glanced over and saw him sitting with the handsome young horn player I had run into at the motel.

Now I knew that Stan wasn't a homo, but why was he sitting so close to the cat. They were practically touching shoulders.

The young guy looked confused. Stan was giving him mixed signals. I knew, by the way that Stan was leaning in and talking, that he was either confiding in the young dude or giving him the inside scoop on something.

Oh yeah, Stan knew everything. All the details about stuff most people never thought of. Where the best climatic conditions were, to grow the bamboo that produced the best saxophone reeds. Where to find the cleanest prostitutes in the world. The physiological reason that certain tribes in Outer Mongolia didn't have any facial hair — you name it, Stan knew it. He was a cornucopia of info, especially when he wanted to impress or connect with someone.

As Stan walked on the bandstand for the last set, he smiled at the young dude and said "See ya later man."

Was it my imagination, or had Stan just given the young stud a come-hither look?

Halfway through the last set, the guy left.

Later that night as I was walking down the hall to my room, I spotted Stan knocking at the young cat's door.

Maybe Stan was a switch hitter. When women weren't around, well ....

++++

Next morning as we were checking out, the young cat came up to me in the lobby. Since we had previously had one or two conversations, I guess the dude figured he had to straighten me out about his midnight visitor.

"Yeah, your boss is one weird cat," the young guy informed me. "First he asked me if he could come to my room and see my soprano. I showed it to him and he played it for a few minutes, then he told me a few stories about Sidney Bechet. *Then* he asked me if I was into trying something. Stan explained how a man could feel intense pleasure by having certain glands stimulated. Your boss was trying to make me, well you know ...."

The cat was starting to turn beet red. I nodded, encouraging him to continue.

"I didn't want to hurt Stan's feelings but I told him I wasn't into experimenting — I had a girlfriend back home. I liked the way he played and all but .... Stan smiled, patted me on the back, said he understood, and left."

A benevolent pervert. I was actually relieved to learn nothing had really happened with the young guy. At the same time I now knew that Stan would go to any lengths to get off.

++++

The band had just checked out and was about to depart for the airport, when Stan came by in a limo. There had been a change of plans.

"The mayor of Greenwich just called and asked me to play a political rally. If you guys want to do it, you can make an extra $500 beans." Stan paused to take a swig of beer. " It's on our way back anyway. We'll just drive instead of fly. Easy in and out."

When we got to Connecticut, Stan was in a completely different mode. He was Mr. Straight-up, good citizen. Father, husband, patriotic American. A pillar of the community. Oh yeah, Stan was a chameleon. In fact, he had what every good con-man possessed. An absolute belief that he was what he said he was while he was saying it.

We spent part of the day whooping, hollering, and flag waving. Then we drove back to New York.

Riding in a limo was primo. Stan always went first class.

Before dropping me off at my crib, Stan scribbled down the address of a T.V. studio in Midtown. He said that in a few days we were doing a T.V. show with Rod Steiger, Claire Bloom, and her husband, James Earl Jones. The bread was so-so but Stan said it would be good exposure.

I called my cousins, Alden and Harriet, and told them I was going to be on the tube. I not only wanted to impress them, I wanted them to be proud of me. I had made it a point to keep in contact with them. Besides being well connected, Alden and Harriet were nice people.

++++

When I got to the studio, a blast of cold air hit me. I was freezing. Why did they have to keep T.V. and recording studios like refrigerators? I was so cold my teeth were chattering. I had worn something skimpy. An outfit that would have been appropriate for a sweltering day in the Bahamas. It was early autumn in New York. Just on the verge of nippy. The fact that my apartment was always too warm had again lulled me into thinking the outside environment would be like like a warm temperature-controlled cocoon.

I felt like I was on the tundra in the frozen north. The rest of the guys had at least worn suits. I was standing over to the side, uncomfortable, shivering and holding a hot cup of coffee in my hands for warmth.

I looked around the studio. Rod Steiger was eyeballing me. He looked puzzled. He probably didn't know I was part of Stan's band. Maybe he thought I was somebody's old lady, or gal Friday. Or maybe he thought I had just wandered in off the streets, hoping to freeze to death.

My thoughts were interrupted by James Earl Jones, who was on camera. He had just started reading a sonnet by Shakespeare to Claire Bloom. She responded by reading another Sonnet to him.

I wondered if people really spoke that way in Medieval times . Or did the writers back then create their own language? The Quakers *still* spoke like that. They were cool — the first pacifists. In fact they were wearing long dresses way before the hippies. I tried to visualize a Quaker. Mmm. Yeah, the Quaker chicks should lose the bonnets. Let their hair go a little wild, and wear just a tad of makeup — neutral frosted lipstick and maybe ....

Someone snapped his fingers in my face. The cameraman was standing in front of me.

"Stan wants you over on stage B. Go around the back," he said pointing out a roundabout way to me, "so you won't accidentally appear on camera with James and Claire."

I skirted the edge of the studio and entered a little musical zone where Jack was sitting in front of his drums, Miraslav was holding up his bass and squinting, and Stan was standing fingering his horn. I plopped down at the 7 ft.-long grand piano.

Stan looked at me. "Drinking hot coffee when you're cold makes you *more* likely to get hypothermia. Your insides never get used to the cold when you're constantly putting something artificially warm inside your body."

"Thanks Stan." I put down my coffee cup down near one of the piano legs. Mr. 411 was at it again.

We played a couple of Bossa Novas. Then I picked up my coffee cup and walked over to the sidelines with the rest of the band. Stan walked over to the big orange canvas-covered couch where all the guests sat and starting rapping with the host.

I thought I'd take another sip of my lukewarm coffee. As I was putting the cup up to my lips, I noticed Rod Steiger walking toward me. I felt a tad nervous. Maybe he wanted to compliment me on my performance. Or maybe he thought that since I was so unusually talented I would be a good person to rap with or even get to know.

I looked up expectantly as he stood by me. I tried to approximate a pleasant expression on my face. A half smile usually worked though sometimes people took it as a snicker.

The cat was exuding radiant heat. He had a quizzical look on his face as he studied my hands.

"I was just wondering, Miss," Rod Steiger said, clearing his golden throat. "How you play with all those rings on?"

Huh? *That's* what he wanted to know?!!

Since I was expecting a compliment I automatically started to say thank you. Then I stopped in mid-word.

"Thank ... Ah ...Well you see er... Mr. Steiger, I've been playing for so long I could probably play with a dead rat on my hand."

Rod walked away.

I hoped I had answered his question.

Doing a T.V. show had been fun. I was sure that working with Stan would broaden my horizons. I would probably get to meet a lot of movie stars and famous people. Maybe I'd fall in love with somebody famous — or, even better, they'd fall in love with me.

I'd make beautiful music, while my famous husband — probably some hunky Hollywood heart throb — was off doing award-winning movies. My sweetie and I would meet up every few months, trysting off the Greek Isles or the Riviera. Then it would be back to the grind, churning out great movies and classic jazz albums.

I fell asleep dreaming some very large dreams that night.

++++

Next day Stan called. There was another gig in the hopper. This one was in Boston at a place called Paul's Mall.

I'd heard of that place. It was supposedly the coolest jazz club in Boston.

I felt like I was slowly creeping up the jazz ladder.

9

PAUL'S MALL

It was a tense scene as we scurried around the Boston airport picking up our bags and instruments. Stan usually liked to fly either in the middle or late afternoon, which meant we only had a few hours until gig time when we landed.

Jack DeJohnette was on this gig, but this time instead of Miraslav (the dour Czech), Walter Booker was playing bass.

I had met Book when I first got to New York and was living uptown. We had hung out for a minute, smoked a little weed, discussed *The Tibetan Book of the Dead,* and listened to Villa-Lobos while staring at my secondhand, faded Persian rug. We hadn't gone the whole "nine" but we had come close. There was a definite attraction between us, but Booker had a very jealous old lady named Maria — a Portuguese spitfire with a nasty temper. It was rumored that she was capable of exacting some horrible-type revenge on anyone she suspected of messing around with her man.

The cat was *definitely* off limits. I didn't want some deranged bombshell, whose happiness depended on being some bass-thumping Neanderthal's ol' lady, on *my* tail.

I had worked some gigs with him several years ago, but hadn't thought about him since.

When I caught sight of Booker at J.F.K., I was taken aback. He had changed considerably.

Once a bit on the pudgy side Book, was now all skin and bones. Besides having a vacant, mean look in his eyes he appeared to be very edgy, his head jerking around every few seconds like he was expecting something. It was quite a shocking transformation. Damn!! Was this Bookers evil twin? I had heard rumors that he was doing a lot of blow, but rumors in the jazz world abounded like flies at a picnic. I decided to reserve judgement.

Throughout the flight, Book had been sullen and moody. Not at all like the gregarious cat I'd once known. I was a little worried about him, though I was hoping his demeanor was temporary.

After arriving in Boston and jumping through the absurd airport hoops, we all set out for our temporary digs.

Stan was staying at some local big-wig's country estate. The rest of us were relegated to the Vendome, a formerly upper crust - hotel that had fallen on hard times. Though the old hotel had a glorious past, it was now a dump. (I was getting to be an authority on dumps.) It was also rumored that Edgar Allen Poe had consummated his relationship there with Annabel Lee, his thirteen year old cousin. Or was I thinking of Jerry Lee and *his* thirteen year old cuz?

The moment I set foot in the lobby, I could feel the vibe. The weathered gold velvet drapes, threadbare area rugs, ancient settees, and lounge chairs with upholstery unraveling were all a testament to the Vendome's grandiose history. The place was a ruined marvel — fascinating, yet now bordering on creepy.

After scoping out the joint and wandering down a few dank musky hallways, I asked the clerk for the key to my room. I then meandered over to the elevator, an ancient cage-type lift with creaking diagonal bars, which you had to push open before entering the elevator itself.

I was so busy wondering whether the elevator would take off while you were holding the cage door that I didn't notice someone trailing a few feet behind me.

"Hey man, hold the door." Booker said as I opened the cage.

After I loaded my bags into the elevator, Book got on with his. As the door creaked shut, he stared at me for a few seconds. He seemed to be pissed off at me for something, but I had no idea of what it was.

Trapped momentarily in the creaky little box, I looked over at Booker and tried to smile.

"Hey man," Book finally said. "Why don't you come to my room after the gig?" His tone of voice sounded menacing.

"Uh, I can't." I answered. "I need to catch some Zee's." I stood there stiffly, clutching my overnight case. My mouth felt dry and my stomach muscles started to tighten as the lift came to my floor.

The elevator kind of jerked as it came to a stop. As the door opened I thought I heard him say "bitch" under his breath. Or maybe it was just the ghosts that hung around the Vendome, mouthing off.

"See ya," I said, pretending not to have heard what I thought I heard.

Book stared at the wall as the elevator door shut. I imagined him sulking, his taut lean face glistening with sweat as he rode up to his floor.

Why was he acting so weird? Sure, we'd had a little something going a few years back, but *I* thought it had ended amicably. When something didn't work out, I always moved on and forgot about it. Apparently, not all folks did that. Maybe this cat was a grudgeholder.

Dammit! The gig hadn't even started and I was having another bass player problem. What the fuck did he want from me?

I lay down on my bed for a few minutes, relaxed, then went over *this* silly new predicament.

I started to remember the particulars of a situation that had happened a few years ago. I had been on this gig with Joe Williams, Mickey Rocca and Booker, when Booker, for some strange reason had tried to hit on me. He took my polite nonresponse as a sign I was interested and asked me to his room, but I immediately put the kibash on *that* notion. Besides the fact that he had a long-standing relationship, I wasn't really attracted to him anymore. I had also promised myself that I wouldn't get romantically involved with any of the cats I worked with. But wait .... a few hours after I'd straightened things out with Booker his ol' lady showed up. This kind of puzzled me. Did Book call her to come down or had she somehow sensed her old man was about to commit some indiscretion? Whatever the reason, I still thought things had been amicably resolved that day.

Was he still pissed about *that?* That scene had gone down at least a couple of years ago. I had almost forgotten about it.

Booker apparently hadn't.

++++

Paul's Mall — a famous jazz spot at the time — was located in a tiny underground mall. From street level, you walked down about ten steps to a collection of shops and businesses (four or five maybe) that dotted a short strip of sidewalk The miniature mall had an arcade-like atmosphere: flashing neon lights, smokey black glass windows, various signs done up in big blocky red and black letters, and the smell of popcorn wafting through the chilly crystalline night air. The jazz club was the first or second facade on the walkway.

Paul's Mall was a much bigger club then it looked to be from the outside. Though the outside looked like a small pizza joint the inside reminded you of an underground cavern.

When I got there, the room was teeming with sweaty overdressed bodies. I pushed my way through the front door and wedged myself through several tightly-packed groups of people, reluctant to part. No one ever figured a short little white girl could be part of an upcoming jazz event, so I was seldom given that extra bit of courtesy the other cats got.

When I finally made it to the bandstand I saw that Jack and Book were already there setting up. Jack waved, but Booker looked the other way. Since it was time to hit I walked up to the bandstand and sat down at the piano.

Just then Stan, glancing at his watch, dashed out of the dressing room and made a beeline for the stage. Tonight there were no stopovers at the bar.

Stan stood on the bandstand sizing up the crowd. He was all sweaty, looking like he had just drenched his head in water. I wondered if he had overactive perspiration glands.

After dabbing his face with a hankie, Stan blew into his tenor, adjusted his reed and counted off.

The music was in the same order as it always was. We opened with "Desafinado" and started going through the book. Sadly, this was the way most high profile gigs turned out. There was no wild musical exploration, no spur-of-the-moment inspiration, and certainly no group participation in the lineup, order, or choice of music. Success was a formula and successful cats oftentimes stuck to that stiff regime.

During the third tune I made eye contact with Jack but Booker refused to acknowledge me. At that point in the gig, I was still hoping our differences — whatever they were — could be ironed out. But in the middle of the second set, Booker turned around and ordered me not to play behind him when he soloed.

"Lay out man, I got it," he hissed as he launched into a flurry of notes. His hostility was infusing the music with bad vibes. I tried to tune him out and listen to Jack and Stan.

After the last set — not seeing any of the cats around to split a cab — I went back to the hotel solo.

The lights were flickering as I entered the lobby. The night clerk had fallen asleep and was emitting loud raspy snores as a moth flitted around one of the chandeliers. The old velvet curtains looked as if they were moving, although the room itself felt as if it had no air circulating through it at all. Fascinated, I watched the curtains the same way I used to watch clouds when I was a child, trying to see if I could discern any real movement or whether the tiny incremental motion was a figment of my imagination.

Suddenly, for no apparent reason, I had butterflies in my stomach. I decided to walk toward the elevator.

Just as I was about to open the cage door to the lift, someone stepped out of the shadows.

"Hi, Book." I said, in kind of a flat voice, trying not to show any emotion.

Book didn't answer. He wrested the diagonal bars away from me, opening the cage himself.

"Get in," He said almost inaudibly.

I felt vulnerable as he walked in behind me, blocking my route of escape.

Booker just stood in the slowly-moving elevator, staring at me. The smell of dried perspiration and aggression was permeating the small confined space.

Book was emanating a bitter, pungent-type odor. A tense-situation kind of smell.

"You're *gonna* come to my room."

"No. I'm not." I said defiantly, trying not to breathe in the fumes.

As the elevator stopped at my floor, Book blocked the entrance. Then as the door creaked open, he stepped aside.

I hurriedly exited the little box and scurried towards my room. I was shaking.

That night, I didn't fall asleep easily. I obsessively went over the situation numerous times, mulling over what I thought my options were.

Maybe I should tell Stan. The downside would be he would think I couldn't handle things for myself, thereby making me a less ballsy player in his eyes. Then again, maybe he *would* understand. I wondered if Book's surliness was apparent to him? Was Stan oblivious to all the times Book stormed off the bandstand at the end of the set or shook his head when he didn't like the tune?

Another option I had was just to ignore the cat. But how much of this shit could I take?

There *was* one option I hadn't thought of. I could threaten to call his old lady. If there was anyone Walter Booker was scared of, it was Maria — the glamour puss from hell.

One thing that I had learned from Pony Poindexter was: if someone puts you on the defensive, the wisest thing to do is to go on the offensive *immediately.*

Time to play ball.

++++

The next day, I went to a macrobiotic restaurant around the corner to meet a drummer named Billy. He had been in the audience the previous night and had introduced himself.

When I arrived, the room was full of Buddhist monks in orange robes, chowing down on brown rice and half-cooked sauteed vegetables.

Billy was late. He was running on drumsky time. I ordered Mu tea and waited.

About fifteen minutes later Billy appeared, all breathless.

"Sorry, the damn phone just wouldn't stop ringing," he volunteered.

I didn't know him well enough to say, "Why the hell did you answer it?" so I just smiled.

We rapped for a while talking about the state of jazz, mutual friends and upcoming gigs. It turned out that he was going to New York for a record date the day after my gig at Paul's Mall was over.

I didn't want to spill the beans about my conflict with Book, but I did ask him if I could stay at his pad one night after the gig ended and ride back to the Big Apple with him. "No problem," he smiled.

As the afternoon wore on, I found myself liking him. I think the attraction was mutual because he paid for my lunch, pulled out my chair, and offered to drive me back to the hotel.

I felt better. Now, at least I wouldn't have to be assaulted with bad vibes on the flight back to New York.

++++

A line was stretching around the corner as I drove up to the gig that night. Stan was happening. Oh yeah, Getz was big. Mr. Info was at his best when he was behind his horn.

I was still debating as to whether I should clue Stan in about Book, when I walked up to the bandstand. I had almost reached the piano when I tripped over some kind of obstruction.

"Damn," I said, flailing my arms, trying to regain my balance.

I looked down at the obstruction and realized it was Bookers foot. Something I couldn't have avoided because it wasn't there a second ago.

"Clumsy, clumsy," Book clucked. "Gotta watch where you're walkin'."

I glared at Booker, but he was looking elsewhere. In fact, he was so wired his eyes were looking in several directions at once. This was definitely not the cat I had once known.

I felt like someone had set my insides on fire. I wasn't smoldering, I was burning. But getting physical was out of the question because of Booker's size. Even at his thinnest, he was a big dude.

I made a decision.

During the break, I walked over to the table where Stan was sitting. He was talking to a lady with gigantic boobs, a French twist, and two tons of makeup. She was staring at Stan, completely transfixed as he hit her with his magic info.

"No, *this* suit is made from a special kind of wool only found in Scotland. That's why the lapels lie so flat," Stan was saying. "Only young sheep fed on a diet of special grass from the highlands ...."

"Excuse me Stan, ... Can I have a word with you?"

Stan looked at me like I had just interrupted him as he was about to climax.

"I'm sorry." he said to the French twist. "Don't go anywhere, baby, I'll be right back."

He took me over to the side and stared at me. He was impatient. I'd broken the, cat's stride.

"Well?"

"Well I have a bit of a problem. I don't mean to be a snitch, but Book is acting kind of weird. I don't know what's with that cat. He ah, kinda threatened me in the elevator last night and ...."

"Yeah, well you're a grown-up." Stan proclaimed. "Handle it! If I had to referee every little altercation, I couldn't concentrate on what *I'm* supposed to be doing."

Stan looked up for a second to make sure Miss Big Boobs hadn't flitted off somewhere.

"Yeah, fuck em' if they can't take a joke," Stan said jovially as he dismissed me. "Tell him to kiss your little ass."

Stan strode back to his lady friends' table.

Stellar advice.

The rest of the night was a Boss Nova marathon. Stan was on a slow boat to Brazil. I was exhausted as I walked back to the dressing room.

As I was about to open the door, Booker appeared from out of nowhere and grabbed my arm.

"Hey bitch, You're coming to my room." I'd had enough.

"Yeah, and I'm calling your old lady. She'll be down here in a heartbeat if she thinks something weird's going down, man.

Now Booker's face changed. Now he not only *looked* mean, he was boiling, fuming, foaming at the mouth.

"That's what I fuckin' thought, you bitch. *You* called her last time. *Now* I know why she came down so quick. Yeah, Miss High and Mighty, Miss Stuck Up on the Ceiling, Miss...."

"What are you talking about? *I* didn't call her. She came down because she knows you. *She* knows you're a fucking drugged-out womanizing, cheating, lying .... What the hell happened to you man?"

What happened to the groovy, mellow cat I used to sit and rap with? I'm curious ... What went down that made you..."

Booker stormed out the rear exit. I realized I wasn't merely dealing with a cat named Booker. I was dealing with Booker plus whatever Booker had snorted, smoked, inhaled, shot up, or ingested. It was kind of like I was talking to Booker "plus."

The cat was out of his gourd.

Zoned.

++++

The next day, Booker Plus (my new name for him) made a concerted effort to stay out of my way. When he saw me walking down a hall, he'd duck into the nearest room or exit the building entirely.

The threat of Maria coming down had freaked him out.

I was playing hard ball.

That afternoon, I went over to Billy's pad and met a few locals — a horn player and a bass player. This old English professor had a grand piano at his pad and we all decided to go over there and jam.

My new friend Billy was a great drummer. He was one of those cats that was born co-ordinated. His arms, limbs, hands, and feet were all part of a well-oiled, perfectly synchronized rhythm machine.

Jamming with my newfound friends, I felt in tune for the first time in a long while. I was playing the right notes in the right slots. No one was scrutinizing me or trying to trip me up. It was almost like playing by numbers. You knew where all the notes went before you actually played them. You could hear three or four moves ahead.

Oh yeah, when you're improvising at your best, it feels as if your body-mind is being taken over by this amazing creative force.

The one trick is to let this musical energy flow through you unimpeded. The moment you try to shape or edit the magical stuff that's coming out, the muse goes elsewhere. She isn't needed anymore.

I was much more relaxed on the gig that night. Ol' Booker avoided even looking in my direction. Intimidation could work wonders sometimes. Stan knew something was up and glanced around a few times, but he couldn't figure out what had gone down.

Book probably still had a bee up his ass about me, but I knew his dubious inclinations were presently dormant. He was waiting for some future time to ding me.

I also realized that working for a Big Dog was a thankless task. Even though one of them might like you or your playing, most of them were usually too preoccupied with themselves to mention it.

Sure, I was making a name for myself as a sideman, but at the same time, I felt like I was on a treadmill, endlessly going over the same ground. I was depressed.

I was even ready to have my cage rattled.

++++

When I got back to New York, Billy stayed at my crib for a couple of days. It was nice to have a smart cat around: someone that related to you on more than just a musical level.

But by the time Billy was ready to split, I was clamoring for my space back. There was just some shit you couldn't do when someone was hanging around the pad — like practicing, writing, meditating, jumping on the bed and screaming "Shut the fuck up!" when your neighbors across the courtyard started blasting Tito Puente at 7:00 A.M.

That same week I bought two Dylan albums. In the past I had written words to a couple of jazz melodies but there was something new out there.

Dylan was cool — cutting edge. I wanted to be like him, doing something completely new and fresh.

After listening to his L.P. a number of times, I decided to try my hand at writing a rock song.

The result wasn't half bad. The music sounded original while at the same time still sounding like rock. The lyric also came out easily. Maybe I had a knack for turning a phrase?

In any event, I was excited. Not so much by the song I had written, (I knew I'd write more and better), but by the musical possibilities that were out there. Jazz had been around for awhile, but stuff like Dylan; Crosby Stills and Nash; Jimi Hendrix; and Cream was brand spanking new.

The field was wide open and I was motivated. Soon I had penned several songs that were to my ears, good.

The depression I had fallen into after the last gig with Stan was starting to lift.

Then, one morning I woke up singing.

I was on to something.

10

AT THE RAINBOW

Bam! Boom! Crash! Bang!

The couple upstairs was at it again. As their bowling ball hit the floor a chunk of plaster flew off my ceiling. Even if they were practicing for a tournament, that was just plain rude. Maybe I should go upstairs and shut them up. Damn it! Susan, my upstairs neighbor was just too petite to handle a bowling ball.

My mom would have thought her pretty with her long red hair, wide blue eyes, and chiseled features. But there was something off center about her. Her old man, Josh — the big brawny dude with piercing eyes — was another story. *That* cat was dangerous. The kind of dude lots of women are attracted to. The kind of guy *I* made a point of staying away from.

The crashing sounds continued for a while. The folks upstairs were starting to bug me, so I decided to retaliate. I put on *Band of Gypsies,* my favorite Hendrix album and cranked that sucker up loud. I figured it was better than trotting up there and giving them a piece of my mind. If I did *that,* they might not feel so charitable about my practicing at weird hours.

I guess they got the message, because they stopped after Jimi started singing.

I cleaned up the little chunks of plaster, then turned my attention to other things.

First, I got some clothes ready for the cleaners, so I'd look decent for my upcoming gig at the Rainbow Room with Stan. Then I took out some manuscript paper and started piecing some ideas together for a rock song I'd been working on.

The song itself was about Texas. But I wasn't quite sure what I wanted to say.

But there definitely *was* a reason I wanted to finish my song.

I'd recently been walking around the Village when I noticed this tall black cat making a beeline towards me and smiling. He looked familiar but it took me a few seconds to figure out who he was.

I squinted.

Wow! I couldn't believe my eyes.

"Eugene MacDaniels. Man, I haven't seen you since I was twelve." I flashed on my mother taking me to this jam session in . Hollywood. Gene was singing, Billy Higgins was playing drums and Wilfred Middlebrooks was on bass. After my mother informed the band that her daughter could play jazz and was probably some kind of genius, they graciously let me sit in. I must have done something right because they invited me to come and play at all the Sunday jams thereafter. Gene was especially supportive and came over to our house a few times to. teach me some tunes. Besides being a great singer, I considered Gene — who'd had more than a few musical hits under his belt — one of my musical mentors.

"Janie. What's happening baby? Gene said excitedly. "I've been back in New York for a few months now and .... Man! I been hearing about *you!* Shit yeah!" Gene paused. "Now here's the deal. I'm looking for new material. Stuff that's on the edge — more Rock than jazz, but it's still gotta be slick. Know any young song writers?"

This was my cue.

"Yeah, well I been doin' some writin' myself lately. Matter of fact, I've been mostly concentrating on Rock stuff. Some of it sounds pretty good to me, but what do I know?" I said jokingly, trying not to oversell myself.

"Well baby, if you write half as well as you play, you might have something." Gene smiled. "I've still got some pretty decent connections in this town, if you know what I mean?" He winked. "Yep, I've got some cats on the hook that need to put some long bread into something that looks legit, Dig? So come by my crib, lay a couple of songs on me and we'll hang for a minute."

Just then a hotdog vendor walked by. Gene reached into his pocked and pulled out a roll of bills.

"Wanna dog?"

"Sure man." I slopped some mustard on the steaming hot bun and took a bite.

After getting his change, Gene methodically folded the wad of bills and put them in his pocket.

Cool demo.

Impressive.

Personally, I didn't know anyone with a spare dime, let alone a wad of bills. The cats I usually hung with were constantly hocking you for bread. In fact, my girlfriend, Emily, expected *me to* buy her subway token when we went someplace.

Perhaps, I should start to hang with some different cats. Gene would do for starters.

Since our chance meeting, I'd been diligently working on my song writing. Now if only I could get a concept for the ditty about Texas. My family was from Texas. Dad said it was a pretty far out place. Lots of wacko's there .... Oh yeah, and the Kennedy thing ...

Wait a minute ... perfect!

I'd just had a flash of Jack Ruby and Lee Harvey Oswald. Then I thought of some stories my dad told me about his growing up as a Jew in Texas.

Yep. "Judgement Day in Texas." That's what I would name my song.

I ran with that idea and came up with a chorus soon afterwords.

Judgement day in Texas
Sparrows gone in hiding
Joseph, Mary, Jesus
Save the hill from sliding.

++++

The Rainbow Bar and Grill was a classy joint, so I decided to invite my cousin Alden and his wife Harriet. This was uptown jazz. Cool, svelte, and slinky. The Rainbow catered to folks in penthouses, townhouses, and houses on the green shores of suburbia. I'd be playing to a different crowd. Even the drunks in *that* joint had bread.

My cousins — who fit in perfectly with that group of people — were ecstatic. They were making big plans, intending to invite all the relatives I hadn't met. It was rumored that a distant cousin named Howard was Gore Vidal's domestic partner. Maybe *he'd* come.

Tonight there would be an army of Getz's at the Rainbow. Maybe Stan's family would meet my family. A giant Getz jubilee.

Since I'd never been to the Rainbow I decided to get there early to check it out. I hurriedly got dressed and ran down Christopher St. to 6th, where cabs were plentiful.

On the way uptown I started to get apprehensive. The Rainbow Room was on top of the 87th floor and I'd never taken an elevator up that many stories. Even going up *twenty* floors made me slightly nervous.

Before I knew it I was sweating and my palms were clammy. I tried to hold my hand steady as I paid the cabby, but to no avail. I was shaking.

I walked into the building telling myself that everything was going to be alright, but somehow my body's physical response mechanism had already shifted into high gear.

I must have stood by the elevator a good five minutes when I noticed the security guard walking towards me.

"S'everything alright, Miss?"

I weakly nodded and without thinking stepped into the dreaded elevator. I bravely pressed the button and watched the door close. I felt slightly dizzy, but it was nothing compared to what happened in the pit of my stomach as the lift started its ascent. Now I was zooming up through some dark vertical tunnel at warp speed. Though I was on floor eighty-seven in a matter of seconds I had completely lost my equilibrium.

As I stepped out of the elevator, my knees started to buckle. The next thing I knew, I was lying on a patch of plush green carpeting.

One of the waiters saw me fall and ran up to me.

"Are you all right, Miss?" I looked up to see a handsome young dude with slick black hair bending over me.

"My name's Carlos. Can I do anything for you?"

"Oh thanks, Carlos," I said. "I'm Jane. I play piano in Stan's band. I wanted to get here early so I could check the place out."

"How do you like it so far?" Carlos said, extending his hand.

"Oh the carpeting's pretty cool." I said laughing as I got to my feet.

Carlos led me to a seat by the west window. The Rainbow Room was one huge circular space with floor to ceiling windows. The elevators were in the middle of this sphere and divided the big circle into two sections. One section contained the restaurant and the bandstand. The other side housed the kitchen and dressings rooms. There was also a bar, situated near the East window, that spanned both sides of the sphere. A few early drinkers were sitting there sipping, smoking and blankly staring off into space.

As I looked down, I saw Central Park. Evening was falling, and the little island of greenery was almost deserted. Who in their right mind would walk in Central Park at night?

I was tracking some horse-drawn carriages along the periphery of the Park, when Carlos brought me a coke.

"Here. This will help settle your stomach."

"Thanks man. Oh by the way can you show me where the dressing rooms are. Just point. I wanna cool out for a few seconds."

Carlos Pointed. I nodded, then looked away and spaced out. My battery was low after pumping out all that adrenalin.

I sat there for a while trying to focus myself when Carlos came up to the table again.

"Mr. Getz wants to see you in the dressing room," Carlos informed me.

The night had officially started. The general had summoned me. I reluctantly marched toward the dressing rooms. Now what?

Stan was sitting in the corner over by a row of makeup lights and mirrors. There were a few empty beer bottles on the dressing room table. His hair was all disheveled and he was sweating profusely. He looked up and beckoned me over, index finger curling like a Vaudeville hook.

"I've got a problem," he said in a low whispery voice. He unglued his eyes from the dressing room table, and slowy aimed his watery blue orbs at me. "I did something I shouldn't have, and now I'm totally fucked up. I *have* to come down. I need you to walk with me.... Wait! .... Now listen, don't make it too obvious. I'll just grab your arm and we'll go downstairs for a casual stroll around the block."

Stan took out his handkerchief and mopped his head.

I now understood about the sweating and all.

"Can I get you some coffee?" I said, trying to indicate I was into being helpful.

"Maybe later. Right now I gotta walk. My wife will be here soon. If she see's me like this, the bitch will divorce me and take all my bread."

"Can we go?" Stan gave me an imploring look and stood up. He was wobbly. I felt sorry for him. He looked awful — pitiful. He grabbed my arm and I steered him over to the elevators.

As we stood there I wondered how in the world he was going to play? Shit, you can't play a horn lying down. Unless you were Jay McNeely or or some other prehistoric rock n' roll icon. Maybe if you were a junkie piano-player things would be easier. At worst you'd nod out and your head would fall on the keys and hit a few right notes. But horn players — what could they do?

I suddenly thought of an old movie about Jane Froman — that '40s songstress. *She* was crippled but they propped her up on stage and secured her to a pole that was hidden under her dress. Ol' Stan needed to be tied to the mast too. Or maybe he could just lean against the piano and hope for the best.

As we waited for the elevator, Stan was still as a stone. He knew from experience that the slightest little movement could catapult him into some embarrassing physical predicament.

Suddenly, the express elevator door opened. Stan stiffly inched his way into the dark cage, clutching my arm.

I felt a twinge of fear. Dammit! Here we go again.

As we zoomed downward, I could feel myself losing my equilibrium again.

The door opened. I momentarily leaned against Stan as he leaned into me. We were pushed up diagonally against each other like a human tepee. I recovered my balance faster than I did on the trip up.

Strolling down the block, Stan said that he had gotten wind of the fact that his wife, Monica, was coming from Connecticut tonight to surprise him. She might even have their two kids with her.

From the way Stan talked, I got the impression that he cared deeply about her. He also saw her as a kind of warden. Stan was a free spirit. Anyone who put demands on him or wanted him to conform to any behavioral norm would be seen as the enemy.

Stan Getz was a study in contradictions. He knew tons of info, while at the same time knowing almost nothing about what effect his actions had on others. He had managed through the years to insulate himself from others' reactions and criticisms. And of course, drugs were the all time insulator.

Using dope was like putting a sheet of psychic asbestos around yourself.

The maestro walked at an unsteady pace and nonchalantly babbled about his ancestral tree. He thought it amazing that everybody in his family had died with their own set of teeth.

"Yeah, I think it had something to do about the soil in Odessa," Stan mused. "There's certain minerals in the soil that strengthen the bone and the roots of your teeth and ... shit!!"

As we turned the corner, Stan spotted a limo with his wife in it. We ducked into the shadows.

"Okay, I gotta get back upstairs before my wife gets here," Stan yelped, doing a frantic 180. "When Monica gets upstairs I want you to introduce yourself, then to tell her I had to go get some reeds. Whatever you do *don't* say I'm here."

Stan was practically straight as we took the express up. This *almost* encounter had given him some focus.

"Okay, go into the restaurant and watch for her," he ordered. "I don't want her moseying around the dressing rooms. I don't even want her to know where they are."

Stan quickly darted back into the dressing room.

I casually stood near the elevator door, waiting for Mrs. Getz to emerge.

Suddenly, the wide aluminum box parted in the middle.

I slowly walked over to her, trying to seem like nothing had been prearranged. Oh yeah, this meeting was purely accidental.

"Hi Monica?" I said duplicitously. She smiled and nodded, simultaneously clutching the hands of her two children.

"I'm Jane, Stan's piano player. He told me to tell you he went out for some reeds but he'll be back before the show. There's a table near the front reserved for you. I'll get the maître d'."

Monica looked slightly perplexed. Then she smiled. A radiant charming smile with perfect pearlized, straight teeth. Monica was beautiful the same way Angie Dickenson was; natural, blonde, innocent, womanly and voluptuous. She could have easily been the Prom Queen in high school.

I watched her as the maître d' led her to a table.

Monica and her two tow-headed kids were perfectly turned out — the template of the ideal American family.

But Monica was from Sweden. A place where her husband Stan was considered a god. To be sure, he was famous here too, but most Europeans considered jazz musicians to be on par with the most prestigious and celebrated of classical composers. Monica had snagged a guy who was considered by the Swedes to be as heavy as Stravinsky, so *of course* it was *expected* that he would have his eccentricities. Didn't all geniuses and icons?

Monica put up with a lot of bullshit in the name of art.

I smiled at her sitting there at her table, secure in the fact that she knew the score. I'd done my best.

I went back to my original table.

Soon, Carlos walked over with another coke. I had found an ally.

"Just holler, if you want anything from the kitchen," Carlos said. I watched him walk away. He was a cut above cute.

"Thanks man. We hit in a few, but maybe after the next set."

Almost out of the blue, people began to pour in. Very fancy people, among them my Park Ave. cousins and a few relatives I hadn't met yet. Then Jack and Book walked in. I waved to Jack and ignored Booker. Trying to connect with him was a waste of time.

In a few minutes there was standing room only. I walked toward the bandstand, making a detour at my cousins' table to say hello.

Stan still hadn't come out. I was seriously debating going back to the dressing room to retrieve him, when he emerged from the other room and set his horn down onstage. After doing that, he walked over to greet his. wife and kids, then speedily retraced his steps to the bandstand.

The cat looked absolutely normal. He had miraculously talked himself down.

Then it dawned on me that people who were users had ways of compensating. They knew how to *appear* normal.

They could be completely spaced, while at the same time parroting the movements, actions, and responses of a normal, functional person. Stan had *that* down.

For a second, I imagined, I'd never really seen Stan when he wasn't stoned. How would I know, or for that matter, anyone else know the difference?

All I knew was that musically, he was *always* on target.

From the first note on, he usually had the audience in the palm of his hand. His sound was warm and human; his phrasing, lyrical, and his timing, impeccable.

Stan was an original.

During the breaks the maestro dutifully sat with the wife and kids. Beautiful Monica looked adoringly at him and hung on his every word. I don't think Stan understood how much his family loved and cared for him. That was sad because it seemed like he needed *them* as much as they needed him.

Some Big Dogs just thought they had a divine right to love and adulation.

++++

The week at the Rainbow Room had sailed by. I'd gotten used to working on the 87th floor and thought nothing of getting in the high-speed claustro-box that took me to the top of the world.

I also got used to seeing celebrities like Rod Steiger, Elizabeth Ashley and Jason Robards in the audience. I figured, there was something about hanging out with musicians that actors liked. Maybe it was because actors *acted* like outlaws but musicians really *were* outlaws and rebels.

Whatever the reason, Stan and pal Jason Robards oftentimes hopped in Stans' limo and cruised around the Big Apple 'til all hours of the night. The two of them were like hungry vampires trying to suck up every emotional high available.

Even though Stan was married, he paid little attention to the strictures and rules of behavior that most people would say constituted a normal marriage. Stan had an idyllic situation, but he took it for granted, like many of the Big Dogs did.

Stan was an interesting cat. But I had other things to think about. I was preoccupied with refining and finishing my song, "Judgement Day in Texas". At the rate I was going, I'd have it ready for Gene very soon.

In fact I was *too* preoccupied with the damn song. On the last day of the gig I had forgotten to go to the bank to get cab fare.

I had enough bread for the ride up but *now* I would have to take the train back down to the Village. I would get in a well lighted car with plenty of people. It was only a block from the subway stop to my crib anyway. Somehow I would make it home safe.

But I wasn't convinced.

Maybe I could borrow a couple of bucks from Stan to get home.

I was troubled during the whole ride uptown. And to make matters worse, the cabbie, gave me a dirty look when I shorted him on the tip.

The night was not starting off well. I was anxious about getting home and irritated about the dynamics of this gig.

Something was starting to nag at me. I looked at the chain of events that had transpired over the past week. Why was the task of walking Stan around the block and telling tall tales to his wife, relegated to me? I was starting to feel like the Jazz Nanny. I didn't mind waltzing the cat around the promenade once in a while, but this crap was starting to be an all-the-time thing. One of those things you agreed to do *simply by doing it.*

Dammit! How do you say no when you've already said yes? It's like telling a guy you've been sleeping with for a few years that you now want to wait until you get to know him better. Who would go for that?

I mulled it over for the few seconds it took the lift to get to my floor. Then I strolled back to the dressing room to hang up my coat.

Stan and sidekick Jason Robards were sipping Martinis.

Stan looked up at me and nodded briefly, then went back to telling Jason about some chick with a size 52 ZZZ, bust.

"Jason, her tits were so big they looked like huge watermelons. She told me her bras were made by some guy that ...."

I made my exit.

I circled the restaurant until I found Carlos. We had gotten to know each other a bit during the course of the week. He wasn't Puerto Rican like I had first assumed. He was from Boston, and his parents were from Portuguese Goa, which is on the West Coast of India. The cat was East Indian. Carlos De Souza was a Portuguese name.

I had planned to give him a generous tip for all the free stuff he'd gotten me during the week, but now ....

I took him aside and asked him for his address. When I explained why, he laughed.

"If you let me take you out to dinner, I'll consider *that* my tip," Carlos said. "Call me when you're ready." Carlos handed me his phone number.

That was the high point of my evening. From then on, things went downhill.

At the beginning of the second set, Stan ordered me to go up to the bandstand to play some solo piano. Stan was three sheets to the wind, snookered, inebriated, looped, fried, smashed, stoned out of his gourd.

I played about three tunes, then looked around to see if the rest of the band was going to join me. Book was standing by the bar grimacing at me and mouthing, what looked like nasty words. I couldn't read lips but I sure as hell could read intentions.

Pissed off, I tried to grab hold of the mike to call the band up, but the mike stand did something weird and slid down to a halfway position. Then the. mike did a feedback thing. A few people held their ears and looked up inquisitively. But most of the folks weren't paying attention.

I angrily walked off the bandstand and looked around the room.

Damn! Now Stan and the rest of the band had disappeared. They were probably in the dressing rooms.

I went to the bar to order a coke.

Maria, Booker's girlfriend, was standing there in a yellow suit, which was so tight, it looked liked she was poured into it. Her spiked heels made indentations in the carpeting as she walked toward me. She meant business!

Her ruby red lips were inverted into a pouty little sneer and her eyebrows were knit together, like there was something she couldn't figure out. Oh yeah! Hurricane Maria was- coming my way. I was in the path of destruction.

Before I could retreat to the dressing room she caught up with me.

"Where's Book?" she said nastily, hands on hips.

"What, no hello?" I said.

The Carmen Miranda look-alike cornered me. She smelled like garlic and Tabu — a perfume my grandma used to send mom and mom would give away for Christmas.

"Oh I think he just went downstairs with some chick in a lowcut black mini dress." I answered. "He said he had some business to take care of. But don't worry, Maria. He won't take long."

Not waiting for her reaction, I turned around and walked to the other side of the room.

Soon Stan, Jack, and Book emerged from the dressing rooms. Maria had a scowl on her face as Booker walked over to greet her. Soon they were hassling about something. Book was begging Maria to keep her voice down and Maria kept turning up the volume. I had gotten her into a horrible mood. Par for the course.

For the last set, we repeated the first set. Something Stan didn't usually do. But he wanted to party tonight. He couldn't wait for the last note of the last song.

At the end of the night (which hadn't come soon enough for Stan), he handed me my check and summoned his limo driver. I was going to ask him for some cash to take a cab, but he was in a big rush.

I was kind of antsy myself so I said goodbye to Jack, waved to Carlos, and walked to the lift.

As the elevator whisked down the dark narrow tube, I had a feeling of apprehension. It was two long blocks to the subway. The side streets I would be taking were dimly lit and unpopulated.

I hurriedly pushed open the revolving door, turned the corner and walked briskly into the darkness. About halfway down the block I saw headlights behind me. Now, I was half running and half walking. Stories my mother used to tell me about kidnapped children drifted through my head. Maybe I'd end up in an abandoned refrigerator.

I could tell the vehicle was maintaining the same distance behind me. I was being followed.

Shit!

I started to break into a slow jog. My breath was coming in spurts. I felt like I couldn't get enough air. I was freezing and sweating.

The car was now driving alongside of me. In my periphery I saw a shiny, black older model Lincoln or Mercury with four loud-drunk guys, beckoning me to get into their car.

The street was deserted and I was scared. There were no doorways to duck into because there's no access on the side of a building except through a window. I broke into a run, the car following alongside me. Suddenly, they pulled up ahead of me and stopped the car. *Fuck. Now* what?

Some guy with greasy black hair and bloodshot eyes was starting to push the door open. As the car door opened wider I could smell alcohol and pot fumes.

For a brief second I had an image of my mother getting hysterical at my funeral.

Things were starting to get blurry. I was aware of the other perverts in the car shouting and egging the perv on. Then something else was added into the mix. Another car pulled up behind the greasers' car.

It was furiously honking.

It was a limo.

The greasers jumped back into the vehicle, slamming the door and yelling something to the driver, who in turn hit the gas and screeched around the corner.

The limo door opened.

"You okay?" Stan inquired.

I nodded. I was shaking so badly I couldn't utter a sound.

"Here, have a drink." Stan said, pulling out his hip flask. "This will calm you down. Vodka. Great tranquilizer. You can drink a gallon of this and no one will smell it on your breath."

"Thanks Stan, but I'm cool. I'll be fine in a minute."

"Okay. Where can we take you?"

"If you're heading downtown, I'm in the Village," I said as I hopped in. I was still shaking.

"Murray. Let's go downtown first." Stan said to the driver.

"Just relax." Stan advised. "You're safe now."

I sat in silence sinking into the cushy back seat as Stan studied my face.

"What do you use on your skin. Your complexion is flawless. You don't have any pores. I know you're young, but your skin is like a baby's butt."

"Oh, I use Ponds cold cream and some stuff I found at the drugstore called Second Debut." I wasn't sure if I should give away *all* my beauty secrets. "I'm also on a brown rice and fish diet," I reluctantly volunteered.

Stan nodded. "How do *you* make the brown rice? I was on a brown rice diet in the obesity clinic in Durham, where I went to lose a few, but I've never figured out how to cook it at home."

"Well, you're welcome to come up to my crib and try it the way *I* make it. I just made a batch before I left for the gig, so I've got plenty."

We rode downtown as Stan rattled on about the fat farm in Durham. He described what a day at the fat farm was like. It seemed pretty boring to me: weigh in, eat, go for a walk, eat another low calorie meal, then watch T.V. while you waited for your tasteless, local dinner. After dinner, Stan explained, lots of people went into town and cheated. He said he'd seen fatties wolf whole pizza's down, or make a double order of fries disappear in seconds flat. Stan, of course, never did that. Uh uh.

By the time we got to my crib I was hungry. So was Stan.

He told Murray to wait in front of my building and walked upstairs with me.

Stan was Mr. Curiosity as he sat down on my lumpy couch.

"Where did you ever get a couch like this?" Stan queried.

In the course of his visit, I explained to him where I got my couch, piano, curtains, juicer, and poster of Krishna that I had mounted on particle board and hung on the wall.

I then brought Stan a little bowl of brown rice to sample. He took a bite.

I was waiting for the maestro's approval, when it started.

Thud. Bang. Kaboom. The apartment was vibrating and shaking, cups rattling, objects dancing around on the shelves, and floorboards rocking.

"What the....?"

"Oh the couple upstairs is practicing a few bowling moves." I casually explained.

Stan stared at me. "At two fuckin' a.m.?"

I nodded. "Well it really doesn't happen that often," I said as the thumping subsided. "It *is* kind of disturbing but ...."

Just then there was a pounding on the door. For a minute I thought it was the police. But what could they bust me for? Shit, maybe they followed Stan and .... I looked at Stan, then bolted down the hallway to look through the peephole.

Standing on the other side of door was my upstairs neighbor. Her nose was bleeding and her lip was all cut up. She was sobbing.

I quickly opened the door. She limped into the living room trying to catch her breath. Susan looked like a human punching bag.

Stan took over. He put his arm around her, stroked her head and carefully steered her to the couch. Then he ran into the bathroom and put some cold water on a washcloth to mop her face with.

One of her eyes was black and swollen, her lip was bleeding, and there were a million little lacerations over her face and body. *She* had been the bowling ball.

"Here, hold this on your lip till the bleeding stops," Stan said in a gentle whisper. "What"s your name sweetheart?"

"Susan."

"Susan, I want you to sit here for a minute, calm down. Jane, go to the fridge and get me some ice."

I swiftly went to the fridge. My refrigerator was so laden with ice, I had to use a hammer to knock the ice tray out.

A few seconds later I emerged with a few paltry little pieces of ice and a jagged icicle.

Stan grabbed the icicle out of my hand and wrapped it in the washcloth he had been using to clean her face with.

If Stan hadn't been an extraordinary sax player he could've been one of those Great Imposters (airplane pilot, surgeon, lawyer, or professor), you read about. A *real* renaissance man, a cat without a diploma that's such a quick study he can get the hang of almost any profession just by observation. Tonight he was Dr. Stan — swabbing alcohol, dabbing little cuts, and gushing forth encouraging words to my poor beat up neighbor. He would have looked natural with a stethoscope around his neck. But after that little exercise, I could easily have seen him in an astronauts' getup or a pilots' uniform.

The evening ended with Stan imploring Susan not to go back to her apartment until the batterer had vacated. Susan weakly relented. I in turn, insisted she stay with me until her old man split.

Satisfied he had done everything humanly possible for his patient, Stan hugged Susan and gave me copious directions on caring for her wounds. He then ran down the stairs, and requisitioned Murray to drive off into the night.

After that incident, I had a new-found respect for Stan. The cat really could step up to the plate when circumstances warranted it.

I also deemed bowling my least favorite sport.

Especially chick bowling.

++++

That weekend I finished "Judgement Day in Texas."

I also found a crumpled piece of paper in my purse with Carlos De Souza's phone number on it.

I gave him a ring.

II

TAKE ME BACK
TO INDIANA

Stan said we were going to Indianapolis to play in one of those Playboy Clubs. Indiana sounded boring.

I could see it now — Stan eyeballing chicks in skimpy bunny suits and high heels with their boobs pushed up to their chins. And those stupid tails! What was up with those things? To me they looked like giant cotton balls. Then again, I always got the impression that those type of women — ones who emptied ashtrays, fluffed up pillows and could make a short little dude feel like a big hunk of man — knew something I didn't.

I was thinking of watching a few of the bunnies, perhaps picking up a few tips. I wasn't exactly a dude magnet.

I was sure Stan would be observing a few bunnies himself. Though he informed me that the girls weren't allowed to mingle with guests or other employees, I knew that wouldn't stop him. This guy could find his way around anything. There was no labyrinth too circuitous for him.

I was glad that Jack Dejohnette and Miroslav Vitous would be on the gig. Miroslav was rude but at least he wasn't menacing like Booker. I would just blow the little Slav off.

Besides, my mind was on other things. The night before I left for Bunnyland I had a meeting with Gene MacDaniels. We decided that when I got back we'd determine which of my Rock songs to record.

Gene had flipped out over my new song "Judgement Day in Texas." The guy was so hyped he actually told me I was the next Bob Dylan. I actually thought that I looked a little like Dylan. We both had kinky hair and bumps on our noses. Now it was just a question of talent and timing.

Gene was planning to hit up a local hood named Tony ("a guy with a lot of disposable income") for some bread so that we could go into the studio.

Gene had lots of ideas for me. Besides playing and singing for Tony, Gene wanted me to dress wild and provocatively when we met with him. He suggested that I let my hair go berserk and suit up in some floor length flowing goddess gown. "Yeah baby — make sure you wear lot's of red and show some a skin."

The visual thing was quickly becoming an important part of Rock. I might as well make use of what I had.

This stuff was definitely a different bag. But I was getting tired of the regimented way the jazzers looked at the world. There was more than one way to be hip.

++++

We had just flown into Indianapolis, but I could have just as well been in Detroit, Kansas City, Shreveport — you name it. Everything was starting to have a sameness about it. One airport was interchangeable with the next. I was getting tired of being a sideman, trudging up and down the highway, so I could make some cat — who really didn't care if I lived or died — sound good.

I was beginning to feel old at twenty. I could see my life stretching out before me. My future — an endless string of hotel rooms with Bibles next to the bed, detachable hangers, miniature shampoo bottles, the smell of stale cigarette smoke (like the ghost of businessmen past), and showers with minus zero water pressure. This was just another day on the road, another Holiday Inn, another dollar's worth of material getting recorded in the old memory bank.

++++

We got to Indianapolis and after checking into the hotel, went to the Playboy Club to set up. This trip, I was one floor above the rest of the band. Now I didn't have to hear any noisy goings on — if there were any. I wanted to work on some of my Rock stuff in my off hours, so I was happy.

The only wrinkle on *this* particular gig was that playing the piano wasn't the only duty I had.

Stan informed me I was going to run the lights. There were two weird looking foot pedal contraptions by my left foot that I had to deal with when Stan made his stage entrance. They reminded me of the old toggle switches of the '40s. They looked archaic, and this being Indianapolis, they probably were.

First, I had to turn out the houselights with one pedal, dampen the stagelights with another and finally, turn on the spot with the first pedal. When Stan made his exit I had to do that same sequence in reverse order starting with the opposite pedal. Stan assured me it was a piece of cake.

So was algebra when the teacher explained it. But when it came to sitting at a desk in the back of the room and actually working out that crap .... Yeah, I was one of those kids who understood the most difficult of theories *while* it was being explained. An hour later — just like eating Chinese — I was empty. Could be, I had some mechanism in my brain that dumped all information that wasn't related to music, men, or shopping.

When we later returned to the club and started the first set, I was desperately trying to remember which pedal was which.

Our trio started a Latin vamp on the first tune. As I looked across the stage, I could make out Stan in the wings waiting for me to dim the houselights. I took so long, he finally just walked on stage. As he did that I depressed one of the pedals.

Uh Oh .... fuck! I blacked him and the rest of the band out. Whoops! Wrong pedal.

I quickly recovered and depressed the pedal that I thought was the spotlight. *Nothing.* I forgot I had to depress the house light pedal rather than the spot. Complicated, like algebra.

Stan had this nasty sneer on his face when the spot finally came on. Of course, my little faux pas distracted me as well. I was torn between correctly playing the charts and trying to figure out the houselight sequence. How *would* I turn the spot off and get the houselights on again? This was a game of mind Scrabble.

When Stan finished the last tune of the set, I blacked Stan out and then turned on the houselights. I had gotten it right. OK. Cool.

Stan looked my way intending to rag me, then, having caught a cool whiff of some female pheromones, he distractedly walked off stage. He practically had his tongue hanging out as he trailed after one of the two-legged hoppers.

Now why couldn't I get that damn thing straight. I had thousands of tunes and licks memorized, I paid my bills on time, and I could learn a piece of music on the spot. Why did a task like this elude me?

Mom used to say I could perform any task perfectly as long as I was interested in it.

++++

Miraslav and Jack were laughing and talking so loud, you could hear them way down at the end of the hall.

"Check mate!" Jack shouted exuberantly. He had beaten the Czech again.

I padded down the hall in my bare feet and knocked on the door of Jack's room.

He hurriedly answered, than ran back to the chess board. Those guys were having their own little tournament.

I sat on a chair near the window, watching the guy's concentrate. After checking out a few moves I stifled a yawn. It was the middle of the week. Being on the road wasn't like being in summer camp where some gung-ho camp counselors had your days all mapped out for you. Uh uh. You had to figure out what activities — if any — you wanted to engage in .... and even when you *thought* of something groovy to do, you were usually too tired from the night before to implement it. Especially something like sightseeing. Anyway, trying to elbow tourists and bus around during the day with a bunch of slobs from Podunk was exhausting.

Personally, I was always too unimaginative to figure out anything interesting, unless someone else suggested it. That's why I was sitting in a room with trays of food strewn about, damp towels mildewing on the furniture, and trying to follow some cheap miniature plastic pawn move a fraction of an inch on a tiny checkered board while I was trying to keep from nodding out.

My eyes were blinking and my head was bobbing when a loud knock on the door awoke me from my stupor.

Jack jumped up and opened it.

It was Stan. I could see immediately that he was wound as tightly as a newly-coiled spring.

He paced around the room for a minute, oblivious to the goings on. Then he began to blather.

"Man, I had quite a time with that mother and daughter duo last night," He bragged. Jack and Miroslav stared intently at the chessboard trying not to respond to the distraction.

"Yeah," Stan went on. "This older chick came up to me and said she and her daughter would like to meet me after the show. The mother wasn't bad, so I figured the daughter would probably be a knockout. I mean, the older chick had a pair of bazookas on her that just wouldn't stop. Yeah they looked liked projectiles. Maybe she was part of the space program."

Jack looked up quizzically while trying to maneuver his knight.

"It was crazy," Stan went on. "Those two chicks brought a bottle of wine up to my room, then completely undressed me, slowly taking off one article of clothing at a time. Man, they were pro's." Stan was smiling now. "The daughter — who had a decent pair of bazooka's herself — massaged *every* part of my body, I mean every *crevice, orifice* — places where the sun don't shine, baby."

I was hoping Stan would stop there. I already knew more info then I wanted to, but Mr. 411 continued.

"Yeah, but now here's the kicker," Stan guffawed. "Both of the chicks started to disrobe. It took 'em awhile, both of 'em had heavy wired bras and tight girdles on. But after they pulled those suckers off .... Shit neither lady had one lick of body hair *anywhere*. They had both shaved everything — and I mean *everything*."

Before Stan went into the gory details, I politely excused myself.

When I got back to my room, the maid had made the bed and put fresh towels in the bathroom. I lay down and went over the spotlight-footpedal thing in my mind. I hadn't been doing too well with that concept. Most of this week it had been hit and miss. It was taking a toll on my morale. Now I had to worry about hitting the right switches *and* the right keys.

Stan had been treating me as if I was some retard. I actually knew the right sequence, but a second before I hit the pedal, I'd always second guess myself.

++++

I screwed up again that night. When Stan walked on stage, boom — I blacked him out. By now I was screwing up like clockwork. I thought I heard him mutter "bitch" under his breath, but I wasn't sure.

I was losing it. It was hard to focus on what I was was playing. Now I just hoped I could get through the gig without getting too down.

That night I made a promise to myself. I was going home this year for the Holidays. I was getting homesick. Tough little me. The chick that almost punched out Pony Poindexter and told Mingus to "jam it."

A wave of loneliness swept over me. I was inundated with this horrible, big, cavernous, detached, empty feeling. Maybe I was becoming an existentialist — but shit, I wasn't French. To all appearances I was part of this big hip cultural click, but in reality I had no sense of belonging.

After the gig, I made a collect call to Mom. I knew she'd still be up because I was several hours ahead of her and she was a night owl anyway.

I told her to set an extra place at the table for me this Thanksgiving. I was coming home, no matter *who* called me for a gig. Mom was happy to hear that.

++++

The last night of the gig, I screwed up the lights again. Stan turned around and cursed me under his breath. This time he didn't bother to muffle it. How could I explain it to the cat that I wasn't doing it on purpose. I just couldn't get it straight: which was on, which was off. and which was on. Yeah, running the damn lights was like a shell game. By the time the walnuts were rotated and waltzed around a few times, you always forgot which one had the nickel under it.

Stan could be real cold, but at the same time I suspect he felt guilty about the whole thing. He couldn't fuck you over with impunity like some cats could. He was an outlaw alright — but he still had heart.

At the end of the last set — after I correctly blacked him out and turned the house lights on — he came over and apologized to me.

"That's alright, man," I said. "I just don't think lighting is my bag."

I took one last look at the club: cliched red carpeting, cheesy round plywood tables covered with white table cloths, and cheap chandeliers looking like ugly plastic Christmas trees laden with too much tinsel. Ugh!

The jazz life was staring to suck!

++++

I hated to be rushed. Stan had called about 10 a.m. and said we were taking an earlier flight. Scramble time. I looked in the mirror and greeted my ugly morning face — baggy eyes, snarled kinky hair and sparse, scraggly eyebrows. I quickly put on my makeup, stuffed my P.J.'s and gig clothes into my overnight case then threw all my toiletries into a bag. Just as a precaution, I looked under the bed and checked the closets. Everything was packed. No stray panties or socks.

Naturally, when I got home there would be a few things missing. Murphy's Road Gig Law.

I tried to run down to the coffee shop, but my new crepe soled shoes had too much traction, causing me to stumble more then a few times on the plush carpeting.

When I got to the coffee shop, it was crowded so — to expedite matters, I ordered an egg salad sandwich and coffee to go. I then went to the lobby to check out and wait for the rest of the cats. I was the first one there — as usual. Damn, it seemed no matter how late I was for any given event, I was still always the first one there.

Could a person be *too* conscientious?

After sitting on the overstuffed couch in the lobby and drumming my fingers on the end table, I finally saw the rest of the band straggle in. Stan was listlessly trailing the pack, looking like he'd had too many extra curricular activities the night before. I decided not to ask.

Soon we were hot-rodding it toward the airport. The limo driver had supplied Stan with a little pillow. He was sitting near the window making snoring sounds.

As we boarded the plane, I noticed it was half empty. We sat on the ground waiting for more passengers to arrive, but when no one else showed, we lifted off.

Stan and the guys sat up front toward the nose while I opted for the belly. Somehow it seemed the middle of the plane was a more spacious place to sit — especially when you were about the only one sitting there.

I yawned and leaned back in my seat. It was an ideal day to be airborne; azure blue sky, fluffy white clouds, and an absolutely perfect view of the countryside. The stewardess made a big fuss over the band because she had only a few people besides us to attend to and we were the closest thing to celebrities onboard.

Sky-waitress brought me several meals, (which I picked at, eating only the choice parts) and got me scores of pillows, packages of nuts, carbonated drinks, and magazines. I stuffed my face and thought about this cute Chinese guy I had gone out with a couple of weeks ago. He had ordered me a whole fish, and I had asked him if it was traditional for Chinese people to eat the head of the fish.

He had laughed and asked me if Americans ate cows' heads? I was thinking of a million clever comebacks, when Stan came over and sat next to me.

"Jane, we're working next week at the Village Gate, but ... a ... I'm using Chick." Then he leveled his baby blues at me.

"I just wanted to be straight with you. It's an important gig and I've got to have Chick."

All of a sudden I felt a surge of adrenalin in my stomach. I could feel the bile rising. I was hurt and angry. I felt like someone had stabbed me in the heart.

It was exactly like high-school. I remembered a time I had tried out for an exclusive sorority called the Debs or something like that. I was rushed by their only fat and ugly member Judy Lutz, who was only a member because her mom was supposedly a famous Hollywood agent. I had seen her mom once — a steely looking woman with brick red hair and huge pointy boobs.

Judy coerced me into playing piano for some of the Debs parties, in hopes that it would ingratiate me with some of the young socialites. I did numerous little freebees until the day of reckoning — pledge day.

On that particular day, if you were voted in, they'd come and pick you up and take you to this soiree they were throwing at some mansion in Encino Hills.

Pledge morning: I put on my spiffiest threads and waited on the steps of my apartment building.

I sat there on the hard-assed cement, waiting and hoping Judy's convertible would pull up to my apartment building and magically whisk me away to this wonderful festive gathering of newly-minted debutantes.

I roosted there until the sun went down. Then Dad opened the screen door and told me to come in. I was shivering and there were tears in my eyes. He tried to comfort me, saying life wasn't fair and folks don't always do what you want them to and all that kind of stuff. Anyway, he reminded me that I had something infinitely more valuable than wealth — I had *talent.*

Those fuckers! I wasn't good enough to be in their exclusive club, but I *was* good enough to entertain them.

I felt that Stan was using me in the same way. I was good enough to work in the hinterlands, but not good enough for an A-team, high profile New York, New York gig. Yeah, baby, take me to Denny's on your cheap dates, but get some ditzy homecoming queen for your prom.

I was silent for a few seconds then I spoke.

"Man, why are you doing this to me? I've worked all your little shit gigs out in the boonies with you .... I think I deserve more than this."

I was pissed. Every time it looked like I was getting ahead, I had to take two giant steps backwards. Life was a a cosmic game of Mother May I.

I wasn't about to back off. Stan actually looked scared.

"Stan, if I can't work the Gate with you, don't bother to call me again."

Stan looked shocked. I don't think he understood my rationale.

Then I saw that he had tears in his eyes. Oh yeah, Stan had moments of remorse, but they didn't last long.

After mouthing off, I wanted to take it back — but it was too late.

Stan got up without saying a word and returned to his seat.

++++

Stan Getz was now a ghost of the past.

I *still* was trying to make the A-list. All dressed up, nowhere to go. A socialite without a ball.

12

MINGUS REVISITED

When I got back to the Big Apple, I was both depressed and enthused. Stan Getz was now part of my past. A bridge had been burned. I was angry with myself. Even at close range, without the distance of time, I saw how I had sabotaged myself.

Still, I had a feeling of enthusiasm because a new musical venue was opening up for me.

Gene McDaniels had scheduled a meeting with Tony — the mobster record guy — in a couple of days. I was constantly singing the verse of a new song I wrote; "Johnny Longone."

Of kingly independence was my father born
Aristocrat of withered lands
Stranded on the middle road of life —
And patchwork miles just lay ahead.

Gene and I decided that we would meet briefly before going to Tony's. We'd discuss strategy, check out my presentation. Then cab it to Tony's neck of the woods — Midtown.

I was a little concerned about meeting the Guy. How should I act? Dammit, Tony was a bonafide gangster. He had the power to change my life in more ways than one. If I crossed the dude I could wind up in wet cement.

I had heard stories about a sax player named Albert Ayler — a freeform, Ornette Coleman-type player — who'd been found floating face down in the Hudson in the early '60s. Same old story. He was involved with the *wrong* people. In fact, Albert was taken out just as he was starting to get somewhere — and *his* stuff (all that honking and shrieking) was hard to sell. Why would someone want to put a hit out on an about-to-be successful investment? I thought about it for a minute then blew it off. If it was my time — it was my time. *C'est la vie.*

The day of the meeting I spent about two hours getting dressed. First I washed my hair, doused it with sugar and water, then frizzed it up with a blow dryer. Then I painstakingly put various dried flowers peeking out of my rats nest. Next I applied makeup that was soooo subtle, it defied detection. Oh yeah, hippies were all made up to look "natural" and being a hippie was pain in the ass.

After that I put on my diaphanous see-through goddess gown, and adorned myself with a ton of silver jewelry:

rings, bracelets, beads, and dangly earrings — *de rigeur* for any Rocker.

To top off the outfit, I put on a navy-blue boy's marching-band jacket, complete with epaulets. I was in full dress regalia as I strutted in front of the mirror, holding my invisible mike.

I felt pleased with myself as I headed toward the subway station.

People stared as I boarded the subway to Gene's crib. The car was jammed, so I stood the whole ten blocks, basking in the eerie fluorescent light and the silent approval of the subway grinches. As I made my exit, a couple of cats applauded. A good sign.

Gene was standing on the landing, watching me as I trudged up the two flights. He whistled between his teeth as he ushered me into his "lair."

"Wow! Holy shit! You're gonna freak Tony out in that get up." Gene gave me the thumbs up as I sat down on his old red velvet antique couch.

"How about some fried chicken?" Gene said eyeing me. "Susan Jane just made a batch — got a special recipe from my Aunt in Kansas City."

I absently shook my head. I couldn't even think about eating now.

Susan Jane, Gene's beautiful young girlfriend looked at me and smiled. "You look groovy," She said knowingly.

"You've got the kind of face that's never going to age. I can tell by your skin and bone structure."

Susan Jane was young and wise. Gene contended she was an old soul that had been around since the beginning of time. Oh yeah, this chick knew *everything.* The girl made you feel comfortable when you were in her presence. She also knew *just* what to say. Whenever I was around, I studied her. Susan Jane had social skills a diplomat would envy. Besides that, she catered to Gene's every whim and never ever made him feel guilty.

Gene scarfed a couple of drumsticks, licked his fingers, and received his mandatory daily astrological reading from Susan Jane. Then we were off.

"Shit, man," Gene said as we cleared the steps. "You *know* I don't make a move before I consult with my old lady. She's got that psychic thing down. If *she* says Tony's cool, he's cool."

Gene quickened his pace as we skirted the sidewalk.

"Listen, I just got a dynamite concept for a new album. It'll be called *Revolution* and I'll have Susan Jane and some of her girlfriends pose on the the cover wearing some funky threads and carrying machine guns. I've already got six of the songs written." Gene was getting revved up. "And baby, you'll play piano and a little organ on it. Uh, wait a minute." Gene spotted a cab and jumped out in the street.

"Shit, those fuckers see a black man and speed up! Wait, here's another one."

A dirty, battle-worn, Yellow cab screeched to a halt as Gene jumped. out in the street again.

He ceremoniously opened the door for me. "Fiftieth and Broadway my man."

Gene momentarily forgot about his record as he filled me in on our meeting with Tony.

"Now listen man, with *this* cat you don't ask any questions. Dig? Just let the dude do most of the talking. If there's anything we need to know, *I'll* ask." Gene informed me. "Let's just see what the cat proposes."

I listened silently, nodding at key points.

"And baby, the more mysterious you look, the more the cat's gonna want you on his label. Be nice but not too nice. A little bitchy works sometime."

Gene didn't have to pull *my* coat. I'd figured out that shit a long time ago. But I guess he felt it was his duty to tell me that stuff, so I smiled and nodded.

When we arrived, Tony opened the door before we even knocked. The cat must've had a periscope. He hustled us in to a bare-bones waiting room with red tile floors and an old office-type desk.. The place had a dark look to it. The blinds were drawn and there were no pictures on the dingy beige walls.

Tony excused himself and rushed into the studio to get the previous band packed up and squared away.

Gene and I spotted a little uncomfortable wooden bench with slats. We sat in silence and waited.

Tony was all smiles as he retrieved us from the waiting room and led us into his super new state-of-the-art studio. He stood there with his arms folded until the drummer hauled his gear away, then began his pitch. We listened to his nasally voice as we sank into the cushy black leather studio couch.

"As youse guys know I got a brand-new 16 track studio — da best!" Tony winked at Gene. "Like I tell my associates, we're in da business of makin' money. Now Gene here, says you're hot stuff. I listen to *dat* guy. He knows. When *Gene* says youse got da goods, that's good enough for Tony. I got dough — I got connections. Maybe we can make a deal." Tony gave me his best shark-toothed smile and looked me in the eye. "But first we gotta get one thing straight. Once I start a project I don't like cats backing out. *Capish?"*

I looked at Tony. He looked like the mobster he was — short and swarthy with a bit of a bulbous nose and a little rosebud Italian mouth. His black hair was combed into a loopy pompadour and his outfit was pure *Westside Story.*

I eyeballed Gene, then nodded at Tony and said "Sure," trying not to look rattled.

When Gene gave the signal, I sat down at the piano and played him a few of my best songs. The cat was ecstatic as we left. Yeah, Tony was into it. Way in.

++++

When I got back to the crib, I was bone tired, but excited.

Gene had made a deal with Tony to produce a recording of me doing all my Rock songs. I didn't really consider myself a singer, but Gene said I had such an unusual voice, that people had to hear it.

I was imagining myself fronting a band and was practicing a few arm gestures I'd seen a few Rock singers make, when the phone rang.

I ran into the little alcove off the entry hall.

"Hello," I squealed, my voice high and breathy, like I had just ingested helium.

"Who's this?" the voice on the other end said gruffly.

I recognized *that* voice immediately. Memories of tied-up pedals, and being forcefully nudged off a piano bench came flooding back. I hadn't spoken to the cat in over three years.

Yes sir. It was none other then the inimitable Charles Mingus. A cat who seemed to be abundantly endowed with genius, testosterone, and pharmaceuticals.

"It's Jane, man. What's shakin', Charlie?"

"Baby, I've got a gig over at the Five Spot tomorrow. Can you make it?"

"You got it. What time do we hit?"

"Ten. Be there a few minutes early. I got a couple of new things."

"Okay. See ya."

"Later, baby."

It had been a while since I'd played the Five Spot — a big old one-story white brick building with picture windows in front so foot traffic from the outside could peer in. The inside looked kind of like an Old West saloon, with bunches of splintery wooden tables and chairs all crowded together, giving the place a kind of raucous feel to it.

Though the bandstand wasn't elevated, it had a rail around it, setting it apart from the audience. Though drunks would routinely hit the rail, it kept them from running into someone's ten-thousand-dollar bass or accidentally flipping the lid of the piano on some poor piano player's hands. During this period, the Five Spot was home to artists like Thelonious Monk and Charles Mingus and considered a jazz institution.

The Five Spot also had a magazine stand on the outside west wall of the club. So you could run out to the stand on your break, get a *New Yorker* or a *Village Voice,* and find out who was playing with whom and where. Then, you could speculate as to why *you* weren't on that gig.

People actually came there to listen or at least to make connections with cats that *were* listening, so the vibe was always groovy.

I was looking forward to tomorrow.

It would be a trip to see Mingus again.

I was so inspired, I stayed up late and wrote another song called "Who Will Look When You Are Gone." It had kind of a repetitive East Indian-type melody that drew you inward. The lyric was about a woman who was looking for God every where but inside herself. The song alluded to the fact that time was running out and that she'd better put a little more elbow grease into her efforts.

Maybe I was writing about myself.

++++

The joint was so smoky I could barely breathe. Maybe I should start smoking in self defense, I thought as I gasped for air.

I was a few minutes early but Mingus hadn't shown yet. Another hurry-up-and-wait scenario. It was good to see Danny Richmond. As usual, he looked quite dapper. Clifford Jorden looked tired. He was wearing a rumpled old button-down beige shirt and carping to Danny about his wife's cooking, when I walked up.

"Yeah man, she can't *cook* chicken. There's always a little pink part near the bone," Clifford sighed. "I musta' told her a thousand times to leave it in the oven a few more minutes — but she don' listen. Anyway man, we got a few minutes. Think I'm gonna go 'round the corner and get me some Tums."

Danny nodded as Clifford split.

I watched Clifford exit the club, then spotted him through the big picture window at the rear of the bandstand, wandering down the block. As he disappeared into the darkness, I turned around and started checking out the audience.

A lot of the local jazz aficionados and groupies were mulling about waiting for the inscrutable Mingus.

Shit! There was Sue. The designer chick who wore big hats, and was a den mother to some of the more far-out cats like Henry Grimes and Cecil Taylor. She was leering at me from the back of the room. I'd heard that she didn't like the fact that I was female and white, but hey, I couldn't change that.

And then there was Le Roi Jones. Mr. Critic. Yeah, he subscribed to the new theory about Sun People and Snow People. Supposedly the Sun People (all dark-skinned folks) had the superior genetic makeup, and excelled in all *their* endeavors while the snow people — ofays like myself — had inferior genes and were relegated to the dung heap of history.

Jones had recently trashed me in an article he wrote for Down Beat. Of course, most critics didn't really have any ears to speak of, so they had to come up with other angles. They were scam artists with the verbiage.

Anyway, I knew from the get go — even before I came to the Big Apple — that I was going to be subject to race and gender type put-downs. That went with the territory. You could be white skinned but you couldn't be thin-skinned.

Sticks and stones, baby!

I scanned the audience for a friendly face. Archie Shepp who, lived across the street and a few doors down from the Five Spot was standing at the door talking to a drummer named Albert. Archie was probably spouting off about Marxism. I had heard that Archie fronted a cell on the Lower East side, but that was probably just a rumor. Maybe he was planning to raft it to Cuba, (which he pronounce *Cooba*).

I was running out of unfriendly faces, when Mingus came through the door. He nodded to Danny and me while he unzipped his bass case, set his bass upright, and adjusted the steel peg at the bottom.

"Where's Clifford? "Mingus said distractedly. "Went to get Turns." Danny said.

Mingus shook his head, then plunked some music down on the piano. After putting his stuff in a neat little pile, he headed for the back of the room. He was sniffing the crowd out. I could tell he was going to "soap box" it tonight.

Something heavy was going to go down.

I didn't notice when Clifford returned so I was surprised when all of a sudden, I heard a tenor sax at the other end of the bandstand warming up.

Mingus heard it too, and abruptly excused himself, making his way up to the band stand. The cat Charlie was rapping with — a professor type with horn-rimmed glasses and suede patches on his' elbows — looked hurt. But of course, Mingus had no use for manners when when he was implementing his agenda.

"Where were you man?" Mingus said brusquely.

"Oh I was just getting me some Turns." Clifford contorted his face and rubbed his tummy.

Mingus nodded. He already knew where Clifford had been, but he loved the role of inquisitor. He wanted everybody to know he was watching their every move.

Mission accomplished, Charlie went to his book and took out a piece of music he was famous for — one that I especially liked, called "Self Portrait." Then he walked over to the piano to show me a chord Jaki Byard had used on the intro.

Mingus doodled around as people looked on, fascinated. The audience ate up every little thing the cat did. Charlie had an aura of unpredictability that wouldn't *let* you look away. Yeah, you might miss something.

After I learned the intro, Mingus picked up his bass and counted off the tune.

All of a sudden, Charlie spotted some jazz critic from the Village Voice walk in the door. Mingus stopped the countoff and called another tune. One that was more politically, ah — controversial.

Charlie knew all the angles. He walked up and deftly grabbed the mike.

"I'd like to play a composition I wrote when I was in the Deep South." Mingus looked around. You could've heard a pin drop. "This is about barbed wire fences, barking dogs, quicksand ... Mud so deep...."

Mingus was on his classic stream-of-consciousness trip.

Very impressive.

"'S'called 'Tales of Faubus.' " Charlie waited a long moment, then counted off the tune.

The bass played kind of a two beat riff, while the rest of the band played a melody that was reminiscent of a funeral dirge with comedic overtones. *Dat-da Dat-da Dat-da da-da-da-da* ....

The melody repeated itself while the same monotonous rhythm continued.

Then a Ripley's, "Believe It or Not" thing happened. A critic from the New York Times walked in. He, of course, trumped the dude from the Village Voice.

Mingus — who never missed a beat, musically or otherwise — silently took notice. He glanced at the cat peripherally and made an instant decision.

Charlie put his bass down while the band continued the two-beat riff. He situated himself in front of the mike, gave the hand signal for the band to stop, then dramatically stared at the audience.

"Things are happening here, in this so-called democracy — land of the free — that are wrong...*evil.* Mingus was getting his preacher rap on." There are a race of people that are subject to oppression, hate, injustice, ignorance — I'm talkin' 'bout horrible things, that no human should have to endure. I'm talkin' 'bout that ugly devil buried deep in heart of the American psyche called racism."

Mingus took a handkerchief out of his pocket and mopped his brow.

The audience stared at him in stone silence.

"Man, I'm gonna tell ya 'bout black children being tortured, abused, shackled by the system. An *illegitimate* system... one that gave birth to Faubus .... a system that won't let a black man take one free breath from the time he's born till ..."

There was a sound of someone getting up quickly and scraping his chair on the cement floor.

All eyes turned to the back of the room as this huge black cat rose and shouted out, "Why don't you shut up, you yellow mother fucker!!!!"

There was a slight rustling sound in the audience, then complete silence. It was like a whole herd of deer had been frozen in one humongous blinding searchlight.

Someone had stolen Mingus's thunder. For a brief moment, Mingus stared at the cat. Then, assessing the situation — knowing when to hold 'em and when to fold 'em — Mingus put down the mike and without another word picked up his bass and resumed playing Tales of Faubus.

It was at that moment I knew without a doubt that Charlie Mingus was brilliant.

The guy always knew what the right lick was and where to play it.

++++

As I lay in bed that night, I thought about the scene that had gone down in the Five Spot. Mingus was the consummate artist *and* he knew how to garner free publicity. He knew how to create controversy, and used everything he had — intelligence, talent, looks, ethnicity, gift of gab, and magnetism.

Now *that* wasn't a bad idea. Hmmm. Maybe I had some shit — besides my talent — going for me.

I was looking forward to getting into my Rock project and expanding *my* horizons.

++++

For some reason, I wasn't getting a lot of calls for jazz gigs lately. Maybe it was because I wasn't on the scene as much as I used to be. Whatever the reason, my bread was running out.

I decided to go over to Gene's and discuss the situation with him.

Gene greeted me at the door with a glass of Susan Jane's lemonade.

"Here, baby. Take a few sips, it'll cool ya out," He said handing me a frosty mug. "Now, what's on your mind, Lady Jane?"

Nervously, I gave him a rundown of my financial dilemma.

Gene laughed.

"Man, doncha know? Tony will straighten you out. 'Fact, let's go over to the studio today."

Gene picked up the phone and dialed.

"Hey Tony, our girl Jane needs a little cash infusion. Yeah, she's hurtin' man. What can we do?" Gene shook his head affirmatively as Tony blabbed on the other end. All of a sudden he broke into a wide grin.

"Yeah Tony. I'll tell her. Listen man, thanks ... I think six months is fair, but lemee run it by our girl ... Okay ... See ya in a few ... Around three? ... Okay, later man."

"Baby, Tony wants you to sign a six-month contract. If the cat don't deliver, you're free — no biggee. Believe me, it's a short sweet deal. If you sign, Tony'll give you living expenses and a little ready cash. Can't lose man!" Gene rapped his big brown hand on the top of the dining room table.. "So ... let's grab a bite, hash this thing over, and head on up to Tony's ... I told the cat around three. Sound good?"

During lunch, Gene explained how the deal was a win-win situation. "If after six months Tony get's something going, we'll renegotiate our contract and get a nice little taste for you and me." Gene wiped the corners of his mouth with the napkin. "If, on the other hand there's nothin' happenin' you're free to go, baby. But you'll *still* be ahead 'cause you'll have all your songs back and a kick-ass demo. That sound good?"

After listening to Gene's stellar advice, I agreed to sign my life away.

After discussing the contract we chatted about putting a band together.

"Gene, I'd like to get some young cats that can play, but haven't been playing that long," I said between bites. "No jazzers, no smart asses. I want kids that haven't heard of a flat five or nine chord. I want this record to be simple — elemental. No slick stuff."

Gene stared off into space for a minute, then a light came on.

"I know just the cats! There's a couple of kids from New Jersey that Tony's been using. A drummer named Joey Rizzo and a bassplayer named Bill — I don't remember his last name. But they're good people and they'll rehearse their butts off."

"Cool man. Let's call 'em and .... oh yeah, I know a dynamite horn player about my age named Mike Brecker. Gotta' use *that* cat."

Gene nodded and motioned to the waiter to bring the check. Then we headed up to Tony's.

Again, Tony opened the door before we knocked. He sat us down in his dingy linoleum tile waiting room and silently slipped into a room down the hall.

Soon he was back with a discernible bulge in his back pocket. I felt good when it turned out to be a wad of bills.

I'd never seen so many fifty and one hundred-dollar bills together, so I'm sure my eyes were bulging when he counted out four fresh hundred-dollar bills and handed them to me.

"Dere ya go baby," Tony said. "Count'em .... oh yeah, I almost forgot."

Tony ran down the hall as I tucked the bills into my pants. A few seconds later, he was back — contract in hand.

"Sign here, Miss Getz," Tony said offhandedly. Tony produced a pen and I hurriedly put my Jane Hancock on the document.

"If either of youse guys run short, give Tony a call." He winked.

I thanked Tony, trying not to make too big a deal out of it, then split.

"So far so good." Gene said as we rode downtown. "Now let's see if this cat has any *real* connections."

++++

That night before going to bed, I reflected on all the strange turns my life was taking. One minute I was going in a straight line, playing jazz with Charlie Mingus — doing what I had come to the Big Apple to do.

Suddenly, I had made a u-turn. Now I was donning fringe, screeching out Rock songs over amplified guitars and getting all my expenses taken care of by some fat cat named Tony.

Was this a mere detour, or was I wildly veering off the main highway, skipping blindly down some untraveled stretch of road where there were no maps or markers to guide me?

Shit, was I on the road to nowhere?

13

MEMORIES OF BOOKER

It was actually happening. I was on my way to making a Rock record. Not in my wildest dreams .... But there I was, turning musical phrases in my high thin voice (which someone said reminded them of a pitchfork) emoting about love, war, politics, and other assorted bullshit.

Though the band I had hired were just beginners, they did an O.K. job. Besides, I wanted this thing to sound raw — elemental.

Things were copacetic. I wasn't having any cash flow problems since I had hooked up with Tony, so I didn't have to work a lot of stupid gigs, or run around hustling my ass off. I could just concentrate for once, on the music.

Though I had originally envisioned Gene singing my songs, he assured me that my voice — although far from pro singer quality was adequate enough to do *my* stuff.

One afternoon while in the studio, I played Gene one of my new songs. When I got to the line; *saltine cracker c'mom' back here, Mother Hen's got time,* he jumped up excitedly and started flapping his arms around.

"That's your name! *What's* your new name man. *Mother Hen.*"

Oh yes, that was *indeed* my new moniker. When the guys in the studio heard it, they started giving each other high fives.

When Gene McDaniel got excited, everyone got a buzz. The cat had his own internal generator. Gene was the kind of guy everyone looked to for advice, support, and comfort. He kept things afloat.

He was also a cool cat to hang with. Besides knowing what to say and do in any given situation, he was *sooo* good looking, you felt compelled to look, even stare at him. The cat was about 6'2", heavily muscled with velvety jet black skin, an impeccably shaped head, and features that were so perfect, only an artist could have drawn them. He was the Genie *out* of the bottle. When he entered a room, the women would say "Who's that?" My standard answer to anyone asking *me* that question was — "Eugene McDaniels, he's taken."

Gene was a god. And if *anyone* could name me, it was him.

Besides, I thought Mother Hen was as good as Country Joe and the Fish, or Jefferson Airplane. In fact, at the time I actually thought it trumped The Band.

Now I had two identities. Jane Getz, jazz pianist, and Mother Hen — songwriter and rock n' roll singer.

I was spitting out songs like I had some super, jacked up, paranormal song-writing-demon possessing me. My output eclipsed anything I'd ever done. Even in high school, when I did hundreds of line drawings of the Virgin Mary, I hadn't come close to the volume I was putting out now. Every waking minute ....

I had veered off in a new direction, momentarily putting the jazz scene on the back burner. That's why I was totally caught off guard when I got a call from Booker Ervin — a tenor player I had always admired.

"Is this Jane Getz?"

Never having spoken to the cat before, I didn't recognize his voice.

"Umm, Yeah. Do I know you?"

"This is Booker Ervin. I heard you at the Five Spot with Mingus." (Booker paused to take a sip of something. Then he coughed and blew his nose.) "I really liked what I heard. Shit, you were burnin', baby."

"Thanks," I said, suddenly remembering why I had come to New York. "I heard you a few times on record, and I dug the stuff *you* were doing."

"Uh uh," he chortled. "Ain't nothing baby. But I got some new ideas. Maybe you could work this gig comin' up at Slugs with me. Don't pay much but I got somethin' in the Berkshires at the end of the month which pays *good* bread!"

"You got it man. Call me next week and give me the scoop.

"Cool. Later baby."

"See ya."

I hung up. I felt a little schizo with two things going in opposite directions. But what the hell. Too much was better than zip, right?

++++

I now had two wardrobes: jazz, hip, cool, bebop, unisex suit type attire, and insane freaked-out rock n' roll gear. There were lots of people out there with dual careers; why did *I* feel so conflicted? I continually tried to reassure myself that a person could do more than one thing at a time.

To bolster my ego, I called up a few of my jazz buddies and told them the trip I was on. They weren't happy with my additional persona. In fact, one of them actually made noises about disowning me. They tried to convince me that I had committed some sort of sin. To some folks, jazz was a religion.

Turning my back on that sacred American art form was like breaking one of the Ten Commandments.

I almost told one of the cats I would do a dozen "Hail Coltranes."

Why did the cats take it personally? They acted like I had gone A.W.O.L. Oh yeah, they were more than ready to lock me in the stockade. Chain me up in some old salty jazz brig, with tinkling glasses, smoke filled rooms, and a bunch of drunk assholes yelling at me to play "Melancholy Baby."

Sorry, I wasn't going. And if they didn't like it ...

Still, just to make sure I didn't rock any more boats, I decided to stop telling people.

Loose lips ....

++++

Booker Ervin was an interesting cat. He was light-skinned with freckles and an expanding middle. One big dude. I think he hailed from Texas. The reason I say "think," was that I couldn't actually get from A to B with him in a conversation. He'd ramble all over the place due to the fact he was always cranked up on the sauce. He was Good Time Charlie personified. Habitually loaded. Still, I dug him. He wasn't a mean drunk. Besides, he was an extraordinary player.

When we were working at Slugs, Booker would slip out the side door during breaks and hold court on the sidewalk. A couple of times I walked out and listened while he pontificated to the neighborhood wino's and druggies.

"Jazz is a state of mind," he opined one night: *"Sounds coming together and arranged in a way they take you places you've never been. Shit, a horn can strike a chord in you like a human voice. Just like your mama's voice calling you in from the fields or beckoning you there on the, front porch, where the crickets are chirpin', fireflies are flittin' and you're drinkin' beer with your ole man and moppin' your brow because the summer heat is curlin' yo toes."*

Booker paused to take a breath and a sip of wine. *"Shit, you can't go to school and learn that stuff man. Gotta live it. The school of life man, the school of life. Berkeley can't teach you that shit!"*

Booker took another sip, and I thought of the record Gil Evans did with Miles — *Sketches of Spain.* The mere thought of it conjured up castles in Spain, and the ocean hitting the jagged rocks on the barren coast of Iberia, You could actually envision the spaces in Miles's music.

Booker was right. Jazz *was* a state of mind.

I thought of Coltrane's music and how, when he played, I could see the bleached minarets, white-domed towers, and hear the Bells of Mecca ringing in some far-off Arabian dream scene. The hair on my arms stood up when "Trane" played.

Booker had that thing too. He Could make you feel the wind whistling through the trees and across the plains. He was like a Wyeth painting. But, Booker caught the real unabridged, America in his *music.* The America that formed the persona of cats like Trane and Bird. Their America was a place of humble beginnings and rich spiritual resource. Oh yeah, Booker could tell a story through his horn alright.

I wondered if *I* had the ability to conjure up anything when I played. Sure, I knew the right notes and a lot of clever licks, but was I "telling the truth," as one of the older cats put it.

++++

My Rock record was almost finished. Tony was buzzing with big-time ideas.

"Yeah, I know dese cats at Buddha records." He said one day. "We'll try 'em first. If dose schmucks pass, den we'll go ta Tetragramaton. I know a coupla contractors on Long Island that press dose guys records .... dey owe me," Tony said under his breath and chuckled. "Stick with me kid."

Gene, who was sitting at the board, getting a drum sound looked up, somewhat uncomfortably. He was involved with some mobsters in the early '60s.

After Gene refused to pay some kind of fee or protection money to one of the families, they ran him out of New York. Poor Gene (who was living Uptown at the time) had ridden his bike nonstop, back to California in the middle of the night. These days he didn't talk about it much, but I knew he was still wary.

I *did* assume since we were doing business with Tony, that, that problem had been amicably resolved.

Anyway, I was still getting nice fat advances from Tony, so I figured .... fuck it. If my landlord, electric company, and the corner cleaners weren't interested in where my bread was coming from, neither was I. Sure, I felt more than a little uneasy about the deal, but I could live with a little guilt. That's what being an adult was all about, right?

It wasn't until Gene took me aside and told me not to hock Tony for too much bread, that I started to get wary. I was glad I had a few gigs coming up.

++++

The week before I was supposed to go to the Berkshires with Booker, someone knocked on my door.

I looked through the peephole.

Damn!!

The dude standing on the other side of the door was gorgeous.

Long blond hair framed a chiseled face with perfect straight teeth and a straight nose. And his eyes .... My God, his eyes were as blue as the Sea of Cortez. He looked like Adonis. Maybe it *was* the God Of Love.

"Who are you?" I said as I impulsively flung the door open. Oh yeah. Maybe Mr. Right-on was knocking.

"Jamie Faunt, a friend of Emily's."

Emily was an on-and-off friend of mine, who had mentioned earlier that she had a friend in Oregon that she wanted to fix me up with. I had hoped this *friend* was better than the guys she hung, with. At the time, Emily was strung out on jazz drummers — the dumbest of the herd, as far as I was concerned.

But as I checked this dude out I knew I *more* then owed her for this one.

"Hi, my name's Jane," I said breathlessly. "Emily told me a little about you. Come on in and sit down."

"Yeah thanks," Jamie said. "Emily told me about you too, but I've been hearing about you for a long time."

"Oh yeah?" I said, wondering if he was *really* giving me a compliment. "Emily said you played bass in the Portland symphony."

"Uh huh, but I'm really into jazz and Rock .... you know, the happenin' stuff." Jamie's eyes darted around, casing the joint. "Maybe we can play one day," he said, all enthused.

As I stared at the wondrous specimen sitting on my lumpy couch, I was thinking of more than just playing. "Sure," I said, trying, without success to think of something clever.

That afternoon, we went out for coffee, talked philosophy (he was an ardent student of Alan Watts, the self-annointed king of Zen), and made plans to see each other the next day.

The next day Jamie brought over his bass and we played a little jazz, then we listened to some of the cuts on my Rock tape.

Jamie was a Great player, but he didn't have that certain edge that conies with being in New York. But maybe I could help him. Yeah, I could show him some cool turns and licks.

Shit *maybe,* he'd work out in my Rock band! Well, why not? He was gorgeous and he could play. The chicks would be screaming then-heads off when they saw *him.* I just knew that Jamie could be an asset for me personally and businesswise.

Before I left for the Berkshires, we had played some more jazz, rehearsed some of my Rock tunes, and held hands.

Jamie had also promised he would come-a-courtin' in the beautiful green hills of the Berkshires. I told him to come toward the end of the gig, because we were booked for three weeks.

It was looking like romance. Love had knocked on *my* front door for a change.

++++

It was springtime in the Berkshires. Rolling hills, fields dotted with wildflowers and trees, alive with fragrant pastel blossoms.

The Booker Ervin Quartet played nightly in a small coachhouse that had been converted to a bar. And on weekend afternoons we played on a little wooden platform in the middle of a giant meadow, groovin' with nature. As for our accommodations, each band member got their own individual funky little room, outfitted with two cots, a dresser, and a head.

Booker's family had come with him, so he got two rooms. He had a lovely wife named Jane and two perfect children with red hair and freckles. They were smart and well mannered. I wondered how a cat with so many angles could have such a straight family.

Little by little, I started to get a little insight into Booker's personality. He revealed himself, not so much through his words, but through his responses and reactions. He would grunt when he approved of something and stare straight ahead when he thought something was bogus. He would also pepper his discourse with little chuckles whenever he said something he considered noteworthy.

I looked forward to the gig every night. I admired him, and what's more it was reciprocal. Booker promised me that when he did his next album, he would use me on piano. Now, I was looking forward to recording for Blue Note — the most prestigious of the jazz labels. Once you recorded for Blue Note, you were truly one of the "chosen."

About two nights before the gig ended, Jamie showed up. I was ecstatic. This was the first time in my life that a guy had made a real effort to be with me. Things were progressing nicely. No matter that he took the cot that I had been sleeping on and relegated me to the lumpy one near the window where the light woke me up in the morning. Or flirted with the waitresses when we ate at the neighborhood diner. At that point in my life, I brushed things like that aside, seeing only what I wanted to.

When the gig ended, Booker gave me several lead sheets and told me to familiarize myself with them. I tucked them away in my suitcase, planning to woodshed when I got back to the Big Apple. I figured these were the tunes he was planning to put on his next album.

Soon it would be smooth sailing, with a Rock record in the works, a recording session with Booker and a real boyfriend, who — if I played my cards right — might stick around for a minute.

++++

I called Gene when I got back to the city. I was anxious to get moving on at least one front.

But when I asked him about our deal with Tony he sounded evasive.

"Jane, we're gonna cool it for a minute. Tony's having some trouble with the boys and can't be reached."

I had a queasy feeling in the pit of my stomach.

"What about the deal with Buddha records that Tony was working on?"

"Yeah, well .... he said he'd take care of us. We've got no reason to doubt him. Anyway he'll be down in Florida for a minute, attending to some business. He's got investments down there. Too bad he had to close up the studio. But it's just a minor setback."

"Yeah, well is there anything I can do to move this project along while the cat's gone? I feel like I get to a certain point then bam — another setback. It's starting to spook me!"

Yeah, I know what you're sayin.' Let me think .... *Wait* a minute! I heard Jimi Hendrix is doing some recording. I know the cat. Yeah, we broke bread a couple'a years ago in Washington State. Maybe I'll give him a call so you can make some bread while we wait for Tony to get his ass back up here."

I was into it. Damn! Jimi Hendrix. Now that would be a feather in my cap.

"Yeah, man, give him a call. I dig *that* cat!"

"Consider it done, baby."

By the time Gene had hung up the phone I was having fantasies of blowing with Jimi Hendrix. He was the *man.* Maybe if the moment was right, I could play some of my Rock stuff for him.

I hung around the crib for the rest of the afternoon, hoping the phone would ring.

++++

Gene called the next day and told me that Jimi Hendrix had gone to London but to "hold tight" because Jimi had already heard of me and would call me when he got back.

A bit disappointed, I put it on the back burner. Then I called Jamie, who was rapidly becoming my Other half. We'd decided to pool our musical resources and put together a rock group — which would start out as a trio. Jamie put in a call to Bob Moses — a great jazz and Rock drummer — for our first rehearsal. Moses, a guy with wire-rimmed glasses and super kinky hair — had a loft, which meant plenty of space to blow high volume.

My Rock band was happenin'.

++++

Gene was pissed off when he called. I'd suspected something was brewing because I hadn't heard from him in almost two weeks.

"Jane, I don't know what's happened to Tony. I've been calling the studio every day. No answer." Gene took a bite out of something Susan Jane had just whipped up. Probably her special brownbag, crispy-crust, Southern-fried chicken.

"I'm gonna call a couple of ladies that are hooked up with Tony's friends and see what the story is. To tell the truth, I'm a little worried about the cat."

"Well man, if *you're* worried *I'm* worried. Shit, what can we do if something happened to Tony. How will we get the master?"

"Well, you see baby, just before we left the studio last time, I had the engineer — just for insurance — make me a safety." Gene paused. "If worse comes to worse — although it's a second generation tape — we can still put it out."

I had a bad feeling after speaking to Gene. My stomach was starting to tighten up and my heart was beginning to race. Shit was going South on me. Was my Rock career dead in the water or for *that* matter was Tony?

I tried to push the negative crap out of my mind and forge full speed ahead — *writing,* rehearsing, and hustling gigs for my new band. At the same time, I poured over the newspapers daily, watched all the local news shows and called Gene weekly for any news.

I was really bummed out when a couple of months passed and there was still no word from Tony, no word from Booker, and no ring-a-ding-ding from Jimi Hendrix.

I was standing in a valley that was way below sea level. From my vantage point even a small dirt mound looked like Mount Everest.

I was in a hole. A good time to stop digging.

++++

I don't know whether I heard it on the radio or someone called me. All I can remember is sitting on my lumpy couch — which now even had a few exposed springs — and crying.

Booker Ervin had died. And what was worse, he had made a last record — but I wasn't on it.

New York was starting to look like the land of broken promises.

To make myself feel better, I imagined that the record label had insisted on Tommy Flanagan or Hank Jones on piano. Oh yeah, Rudy Van Gelder (the Blue Note maven) had fashioned Blue Note as an exclusive black male jazz label and I wasn't a member of *that* club.

I wondered if I would ever be. It seemed liked I was so close, yet not close enough.

I was jealous and heartbroken at the same time. Yeah, I was kind of at an emotional impasse.

Unhappily, when someone died you couldn't give them a piece of your mind or call them on their shit. That was always a problem. So when I did my nightly meditation, I said goodbye to Booker Ervin and told him — in a nice way of course — how disappointed I was that I wasn't on his final album. Then I wished him a safe journey.

That was the best I could do.

He was too young to have left a legacy and too old to have abused his body the way that he did. Oh yeah, Booker was sprinting toward middle age when he should have been walking. The cat just thought he was having fun — but his body didn't get the message.

14

"JIMI"

Jimi Hendrix had finally called. He had a million questions. Did I play electric piano? Did I like his music? Did I need lead sheets? Would I mind being recorded at the rehearsal? And on and on. For starters I told him I had just bought a brand new Wurlitzer, loved his groove, had a good ear, and shit yeah — turn on the tape machine.

I was way ahead of the game.

Jimi wanted to go in a jazzier more "outside" direction, but he also wanted someone who played electric piano and could "rock." I fit the bill. I was a recognized jazz player who was experimenting with Rock.

After a brief rap, I agreed to rehearse with him and his band.

By this time, Hendrix was a superstar. He had hit the charts with mega hit after mega hit a few years back. Now he could write his own ticket. I was curious as to how much of the Hendrix myth was hype and how much was raw talent. I'd only seen him perform once on T.V. and he looked pretty authentic to me — but the tube was one dimensional. Now I would see for myself.

I was excited as I dialed Jamie's number.

"Guess, what man," I said in a frantic whisper. "I'm rehearsing with Jimi Hendrix tomorrow."

"No shit!" Who's he usin' on bass?" Jamie said.' He sounded slightly jealous.

"Oh man, I don't even know the cat. I can't ask him that." Anyway, I think he's using Buddy Miles on drums."

For a moment there was pregnant silence on the other end of the line. Jamie was a nice guy, but as I was finding out, no one had informed him it was the '60s. Women weren't under men's thumbs any more. Uh uh. Supposedly, there were no more iron-fisted-calling all-the-shots-bring-me-my-slippers-and-pipe type dudes anymore. Hey, I had my own career, he had his. That was my take on it.

I had no intention of getting Jamie on this gig. Shit, I wasn't even really on it *myself.* Besides, I had worked, sweated, and taken a ton of shit to earn my rep. This cat had only been in the Big Apple a couple of months. Let *him* pay some dues.

On second thought, I *did* want a boyfriend and a partner in crime, so maybe I would check out the situation when I got there.

"Well man, I'll see what's shakin' when I get there," I said lamely. Jamie cleared his throat — a sign he wasn't happy.

"Thanks." Jamie said dejectedly. "Wanna get together later? I got the names of some managers from Bob Moses. I want to check them out with you before I call them."

Jamie had practically taken over the business side of my career. From the day I had found out that there was a good chance that Tony wasn't coming back to New York — except perhaps in a body bag — Jamie had run with the ball.

++++

It was strange the way I'd found out about Tony.

I had run into a tiny little restaurant on 6th street to get out of the rain and get a cup of Java. By sheer coincidence I plunked myself down in a booth with a page of yesterday's newspaper on the empty portion of seat next to me. I briefly glanced at it then looked away. All of a sudden, my mind did an instant replay. I looked down a second time.

Staring up at me was a blurry picture of a dead body with the headline: MAN FISHED OUT OF BAY NEAR MIAMI RESORT.

I couldn't be sure but the "yet unidentified body" looked a lot like Tony. Holy shit!! Even in death, the cat projected a certain identifiable something.

Just to make sure I wasn't venturing into fantasy land, I called Gene.

"Hey man, did you check yesterday's paper, front page?"

"Yeah," Gene said softy. "I think it *was* him. Just be careful, man. The cat gave you a big cash advance. I just hope he didn't keep any records. Susan Jane said there's danger around both of us. She did a Tarot reading *and* a psychometry thing, with Tony's gold pen. Yeah, I accidentally put it in my pocket. Shit, I'm lucky I had it. So be cool. My lady feels there's something nasty afoot. *I* don't really think anything's going to happen, but keep your eyes open. Old Tony may be gone but his goons are still around."

"Okay." I whispered, remembering there were evil forces with big ears out there.

Well, that was that. At least I had Jamie, who was more than just a little ambitious.

Right then and there I made a decision. Yep, for the sake of love *and* safety he would — from this moment on be my all-night, every-night man.

++++

Before the rehearsal with Jimi, I practiced my butt off. I went through my whole repertoire of licks from Charlie Parker to

Crosby Stills and Nash. Then, just in case, I took out some lead sheets of my original material. I didn't want to be caught empty handed if Hendrix liked the way I played and asked me if I did any writing.

The winter wind was whipping around the corner as I hoofed it to Jimi's crib. It was a cold ten blocks at a fast clip. I had waited for a bus but after a few minutes had elapsed I decided to go on foot. Who knew when that stupid downtown bus would show up?

Out of breath, I loped up to a stylish white brick house on Tenth St. and rang the bell. I was buzzed in the building by some skinny red-headed dude who said he was recording Jimmy. He silently led me upstairs to a small airless room with no windows, where a set of drums had been set up. Hidden away in a corner was a four-track with several boxes of tapes stacked next to it on the floor. There were also a bunch of mikes strategically set up in the room.

I sat hypnotized by the red metallic sparkles on the drum kit when Jimi Hendrix walked in.

Before I could speak, Jimi extended his hand.

"Nice to meet you, Jane. I've heard good things about you."

Jimi was a soft-spoken dude. He was more than just polite. He was nice. For real.

"I'm looking forward to hearing some of your new stuff," I said reverently. "I *really* dug your Band of Gypsies album."

Jimi smiled and looked away.

For a second I studied him. He looked exactly like he did on his album covers with somewhat commanding features and wild kinky hair. But more than looks, his vibe spoke volumes about him. His being encompassed the whole circumference of the room. He filled up *all* the empty space. That's the only way I can describe it. It was hard to keep from looking at him. It was almost like some freak, maybe a chick with humongous boobs or a guy with two heads was sitting across from you. No matter what you did, you couldn't *not* look.

Mingus had some of the same vibe, but Hendrix had it multiplied exponentially.

I tried to get my wonderment in check, forcing myself to look away. I was staring at the ceiling when Buddy Miles walked in, drum stool in hand.

I felt a wave of relief. He was just an ordinary cat.

"Hey, man. Jimmy was telling me about you," Buddy said. "Let's get it on. Put on the pots baby ... Shit, where's Billy? That fucker's always late!"

A second later Billy Cox walked in with his Fender.

Without another word Jimi tuned up his guitar (a vintage Gibson hollow body that he was experimenting with) while I sat down at the old Wurlitzer electric piano.

Time to Rock and Roll.

Jimi played a little repetitive riff for the intro, then launched into a sixteen-bar blues. His stuff still had that Jimi Hendrix sound but because of the hollow body he was playing, it sounded mellower. Though Jimi was still using standard type chords, he had figured out a few *real* hip substitutions. Everything Jimi Hendrix did was hip.

After a few times through the tune, I came up with a cool part. I copied the lick he played, put it up a third and used it as a vamp (repetitive lick) that echoed the melody.

Jimi dug it. I could tell because he turned around and said "yeah."

The tune was a little funkier than his earlier stuff but not as "jazzy" as I expected. I think Jimi loved jazz but didn't quite have the concept yet. That was cool. I dug the guy's spirit.

The rest of the tunes were basically the same. Kinda jazzy with some touches of R and B in them. A forerunner to Sly and the Family Stones.

The thing about Jimi Hendrix was that he could take the same ol' ordinary stuff and by virtue of his voice and unique way of playing, turn it into something extraordinary — totally his own.

Oh yeah, when Jimi cat started singing, I floated into the stratosphere. This was the reason people loved him. He *was* great. He transported you. When he played the guitar, it was with complete abandonment. I'd seen cats cleverly measure their phrases and meticulously construct their solos, but Jimi just let it rip — and it *still* came out perfect. No thought. He was in that enviable place, where he could do no wrong. The way he heard a phrase *and* executed it was absolutely perfect.

At the end of the session (which was recorded and probably floating around today) Hendrix wanted to rap.

"Man," Jimi said offhandedly, "sometimes when you come up with something people really dig, they expect you to repeat yourself. Lotsa times I feel like I'm in a rut — like I'm spinning around on some treadmill, gettin' nowhere fast. Yeah, don't think I'm not grooved about being successful but...." For a moment Jimi looked off into the distance. "Well you know, what I'm sayin ...."

I did indeed. Though I was trying to get into the particular Rock n' Roll rut Jimi was trying to get out of.

He didn't talk much about his personal life outside of referring to a "problem" he'd been having. I assumed it was drugs, but I didn't want to seem like some kind of inquisitor, so I just smiled and nodded.

Before I got up to leave, I casually mentioned I'd been writing some Rock songs.

His eyes brightened. "I always like to hear other people's stuff. Gives me ideas."

I sat down at the piano and shyly eased into a song called "He's Alive and Remembers."

He's alive and remembers a time when his glory had shown like the stars

Enshrined in the foothills with posters and handbills and an ex

Northern crewman who swore that he knew him.

Synthetic lights shining like bright August moons.

The gods must be jealous, oh give them some room.

The song was about some sixties self-styled Timothy Leary-type, drug guru.

Jimi got it immediately. By the end of the song his eyes were closed and he was grooving to the music.

"Man, I love that," Jimi said. Play me some more."

I launched into about six of my best tunes. One of them was called "Heavens On The Ground Floor."

Lived on a ten mile Baptist highway where I spent my virgin years

Giving door to door excuses, 'til the Saviour could appear.

Never had no carnal knowledge, never smelled a bad cigar

Thought they took you to heaven in a pickup truck and that the Lord played lead guitar.

Before I had finished the first verse, Jimi had picked up his guitar and was playing along with me.

"Man that song's catchy," Jimi said. "Lemme think a minute. Jimi scrunched his brow and looked up at the ceiling. "You know, I know a few managers that would love to hear your stuff. Baby, you have a way with words .... You gotta get out there girl. People need to know who you are .... Damn ...."

I was speechless. One of the greatest cats in the world loved my stuff. On yeah, he *more* than gave me a compliment. He stroked me in long luxurious strokes. This was the shot of confidence I needed. I was walking on, air as I went back to the crib. If it was freezing out, I didn't notice.

++++

The next day I went back to the studio to do some more rehearsing and recording. Jimi didn't seem quite as with it as he had on the previous day. In fact, he seemed removed from the whole scene.

He didn't quite fill the room either. His aura had shrunk to almost normal size. He was still Jimi, but he wasn't JIMI — the remarkable, unparalleled, magnetic personage with no peer. Uh, uh.

Hendrix smiled and was polite, but he acted as if he were some waiter who had forgotten what I'd ordered the previous day. Yeah, I was just another customer. We played through a few more of his tunes, but Jimi hardly noticed what I played. He was distracted. Detached.

Life seemed to do this to you. Just when you thought things were in line, your ducks were all in a row, things were moving right along and if you just kept going, you could predict the outcome .... Boom .... something happened. Some shit, right out of the blue — something you didn't factor in. figure on, or even conceive of, rolled in like a giant Tsunami to push you off in a different direction.

Today, Jimi was a stranger. I had planned to ask him to help me find a record label or a manager. But now ....

Another stone wall. We did a little more recording that day, but Jimi was neither elated or depressed about the music that had just gone down. He was in another zone! Gone. Nobody home. Out of town.

It just didn't seem like I'd connected with him the other day. Maybe he was a Gemini. I'd probably been interfacing with his other twin. Who the hell knows?

He left before the rest of the band had packed up. As he split, he turned to me and said his manager would call me tomorrow about the next session.

That night the red-headed guy who had answered the door called to tell me tomorrow's session had been canceled and he'd call me when they rescheduled. I could have predicted that one.

++++

A few months later Jimi drowned in a bathtub in London. There was a ton of mystery surrounding his death. I felt very sad and was sorry I never — in some capacity — hooked up with him. But I was sure that when the moment of departure came for Jimi, he was somewhere else. Oh yeah, The man was already in the zone.

++++

My connections had disappeared. Tony was gone. Jimi was gone, but fortunately, Jamie was haulin' ass. The cat was burnin' when it came to hooking things up. Our little Rock band was shreddin' and we were getting bookings left and right. Jamie had also starting calling managers and record labels. The dude left no stone unturned.

We had moved in together and gotten into a .daily groove. Since Jamie didn't feel he was getting enough playing gigs, he borrowed a book from the library on piano tuning. He practiced on a friend's old piano, then hung out a shingle.

Inside of about three weeks, Jamie was raking in the bread. Together we were rollin' in small change — paying the rent *and* eating out once or twice a week. Jamie had ambition; I had musical know how. Together, there were unlimited possibilities — as long as we could get along.

But getting along took a back seat to getting ahead for Jamie. He was way too singular to be part of a twosome —

but I shut my eyes to the telltale signs. We plotted, planned and visualized how we would launch our ship. Then we'd eat, sleep, and dream about getting out there. Two driven people joined at the hip by ambition.

As far as will power went, Jaime was formidable and I was no quitter either. We'd leave the personal problems for some other time.

By now, I was resigned to the fact that my life and career were going in another direction than originally planned. But hey, what better time to change horses than in midstream.

15

LAST JAZZ GIG

Charles Lloyd had called. He was in desperate straits and needed a piano player and bass player for a gig in Indiana. I gave him the skinny on my old man.

"Can he play, baby?" Charles inquired.

"Yeah Jamie can play," I said somewhat tentatively.

I knew that if Jamie thought I had recommended someone else, he'd be one very angry dude. Jamie could be irritatingly stubborn and single-minded. His personality had about as much flex as a steel brace.

I wasn't altogether sure that Charles would like Jamie's playing, but I figured since I was slowly inching my way out of the jazz world, it really didn't matter too much *what* Charles thought. Besides, Charles Lloyd was a *really* eccentric cat. You never really knew in advance what his reaction to any given thing would be. The dude was chock full of surprises.

I had gotten a first-hand glimpse of Charles earlier in the year doing an Asian tour with him, traipsing around a half dozen humid countries with palm trees, ancient buses and culinary, surprises. You know, stuff that *tasted* like chicken but wasn't *really* chicken.

Charles Lloyd was a study in contradictions. For a cat that professed to be spiritual, he wholeheartedly embraced every vice that crossed his path. In fact, he never met a vice he didn't like-though I think he probably laid off the hard drugs.

Getting a straight answer out of Charles was also a problem. Talking to him was like going one-on-one with a pinball machine. His thoughts shot out at you like those lightning-fast balls you tried to maneuver by tilting the pinball machine and frantically swerving the side lever. But despite your best efforts the balls always rolled back willy-nilly into their mechanical orifice without hitting the designated target — or in Charles's case, the point.

Charles Lloyd played great, but you never really got the feeling he liked the music. He spoke in a jazzy, hip kind of monotone which oftentimes made his patter hipper than his musical groove.

In any event, I got Jamie on the gig, hoping Charles would at least think he was decent.

Jamie was stoked at the thought of playing with Charles Lloyd, and immediately started calling friends and relatives in Portland. *Now* Jamie's homies would think the cat was into some heavy shit. But I didn't care. For all Jamie's braggadocio and posturing, the cat took care of business. At times, he seemed to have my best interests at heart.

Before we left for Indianapolis, Jamie had made appointments with a few managers. Some of these cats were heavy hitters with serious track records. Cats that had gotten groups like Cream, Strawberry Alarm Clock, and Buffalo Springfield up and running.

One of the guys we interviewed was Lee Housekeeper. He was a dude in his late twenties who had already put together a few deals and knew the ropes. When he heard my songs, he flipped. To Lee, I was some strange frizzy-haired, charismatic genius. Of course, that was the effect I was trying to create. Part of being a successful Rocker was having the mystique thing down. Now, *not* knowing what to say was an asset. The formula was simple: the more mystery projected, the more interest generated.

I liked Lee because he had a million ideas on how to market me and my music. We even spent a whole day, trying to figure out what I should call my group. Lee liked "Mother Hen" but wanted to check out a few other options. He suggested using my first name as the group name. At the time I thought the name "Jane" was a loser.

Looking back now ....

After interviewing about five more cats, Jamie and I called Lee back and told him to hang tight; it was looking good for him. We promised to give him a definite answer after we came back from Indianapolis.

The night before we left, Lee took me to a party at Laura Nero's penthouse, an aery hippy retreat perched atop of a grand, old brick building on the Upper West Side. Laura had just written a couple of tunes I really liked — "There's a Rose in Spanish Harlem" and "Stone Soul Picnic."

Laura looked both artsy and sultry in her long flowing white robes and raven locks. She had a kind of ethereal, not quite there quality about her that was intriguing. But underneath it all, I could tell she was savvy. Her eyes surreptitiously darted about the room checking out all the folks and pinpointing their activities. Nothing escaped *that* chick.

Her crib was done up in '60s paraphernalia — white-lantern type lamps with tie-dyed scarves draped over them, hundreds of flickering candles, and velvet and paisley floor pillows. Scattered about were a few desultory pieces of borrowed patio furniture. I noticed a little solitary used spinet situated in the corner. It was the type of inexpensive piano a child usually gets as their first instrument.

I snickered. Why, with all her bread, didn't she have a grand piano? I would have opted for a Steinway B. Well maybe she just had that piece of junk for effect. On second thought, after eyeballing her stuff, or lack thereof, it didn't look like she had given it a thought one way or the other.

I vowed — if I ever got anywhere — I'd buy a groovy piano. *I* personally considered a piano much more then just a "piece of furniture."

++++

I don't know whether I consciously knew that the gig with Charles Lloyd would be my last jazz gig. The whole thing — plane ride, hotel, even the gig itself, had the feeling of a non-event.

The trip to Indianapolis was on par with a trip to the corner deli.

After Charles made a few remarks to Jamie about the "feel" his tunes were supposed to have, we never heard another peep from him. Charles was elusive and Jamie was elusive too. They were dudes with lofty thoughts who didn't want to expend the energy to co-mingle their insightful perceptions.

Too Zen for me.

Looking back, I would probably liken that final jazz gig to someone's last day on earth.

The day would start off the same as every other day. You'd brush your teeth, make a few phone calls, pick up your mail, grab a cup of coffee at the corner coffee shop, and proceed to take care of all the other bullshit.

Then suddenly, somewhere in the day's routine, a runaway car, a stab of pain in the chest, a gunshot ... something would happen. But before you could even contemplate the catastrophic event that had befallen you, it would be all over. Boom!

In the blink of an eye my jazz days were over.

++++

When Jamie and I got back to New York, things were moving fast. Lee Housekeeper (who had taken control of the ship in our absence) had contacted at least six record labels. They were all interested. I was becoming a hot property.

"Why don't we start a bidding war?" Lee said to me one morning as we were discussing various strategies. "We could jack your price up sky high, then give you to the highest bidder."

"What about promotion?" I asked. (Record promotion was the name of the game. Without a push from your record company, your product would die on the shelves, or even worse, never arrive.)

"Well, we'll see if we can't get some guarantees in the contract about that. Man, that cat from R.C.A. was *droolin'* when he saw your picture. Yeah, the vice president of R.C.A's. got a thing for you. Of course, there's a few smaller labels out there that want you too. They might not be able to give you as big an advance as R.C.A. but they *might* be better for your career."

It was hard to know what to do. On the one hand, I'd been struggling for a few years now and a big payday looked like the best bet. No more third rate hotels, cheap little greasy diners, buying shit on sale that had been picked over, mauled and had threads starting to unravel. On the other hand, that same big label could give you a huge advance, then take your product and bury it, claiming it was a tax write-off. You'd be back to square one, career wise. Of course, you'd still be a few bucks richer.

I wanted to take some time out and give the matter some serious thought, but there was too much going on.

Jamie's parents were coming to town and he was conflicted about his parent's knowing we were shacked up. He contended that his folks — who were devout Christian Scientists would be all bent out of shape if they thought that their son was living "in sin."

Even my mom, who was some rich guy's mistress, was a little concerned. She didn't want me to end up like her — a gal who couldn't get a guy to close the deal. After a long discussion, Jamie and I concluded we had only one choice. We had to tie the knot. It was time for a long white dress, ice on my finger, and a license to merge.

About two weeks before Jamie's parents arrival, we sent out funky little hand-written invitations. The wedding was to be held on Park Avenue at Alden and Harriet Getz's large, luxurious eight room apartment.

++++

R.C.A. had taken the bait. They had to have me, outbidding everyone else — including Warner Brothers — by $25,000.

Right in the middle of planning the wedding, my ship had come in. And baby, it was a *rocket-ship.* I was getting $100,000 bucks to produce two records plus a $40,000 cash advance for the first record and a $30,000 advance for the second.

Lee figured that about a week after the marriage ceremony, the lawyers would have the contracts done. When I called Alden and Harriet with the news, they offered up their superior digs for a catered dinner/contract signing. Having my wedding at their digs was cool enough but they had outdone themselves by letting us close the R.C.A. deal there.

I hoped, once those R.C.A. execs got a whiff of my relatives' status, they'd be reluctant to fuck with me.

I must've been dreaming.

++++

Mom arrived a week before the wedding. Jamie and I picked her up at the airport. She looked much older and more world weary then I had remembered.

When she met Jamie, I could see an alarm go off in her head. Though she pretended to smile at my intended, a kind of steely look crept across her face. Mom never let on but she knew the score. This was no match made in heaven.

After catching up on the latest non-events happening in sunny Cal, Mom and I set to work looking for a wedding dress. I planned to wear a little ruffled Mexican fiesta outfit — something the hippies had recently adopted into their crazy wardrobe lexicon.

I quickly found a long ruffled skirt and blouse in white cotton. Though Mom wanted something more traditional, I wasn't into it.

Jamie's parents arrived a few days after Mom. Though Mom stayed at Alden and Harriet's place, Jamie's folks stayed at a hotel a few blocks from our crib. *Perilously* close.

Then Jamie did something that was uncool. The cat actually pretended he didn't live with me. Every time his parents arrived at my pad, Jamie would show up about five minutes later, acting like he just gotten there.

It was then I started noticing how Jamie always maneuvered situations, so as to put himself in a good light.

Little things were beginning to bug me. It wasn't that Jamie was a bad cat. It was just that he was singular — out for *numero uno*. But it was too late to change plans — as far as hooking up with him. The train had already left the station and was rollin' full speed ahead!

++++

Alden and Harriet's living room was jam packed. Not only did *my* friends come for the wedding but scores of distant relatives that I'd never met or heard of. Alden and Harriet's rationale was that the more relatives came, the more cash Jamie and I would collect. In fact, Alden had stuck a small table near the door with a big round platter for all the relatives' wedding donations. It reminded me of the omnipresent tip jar on. some of the gigs I worked. But today I didn't have to play "Strangers in the Night" for those few extra *pesos.*

On a whim I had invited my ex roommate, Renee. As we embraced, she pulled out some pictures of her cat, Pasha, and tried to make believe she was happy, but she was as discontent as ever. I wondered why I had been so jealous of her a few years back. Now I was sorry about moving out so abruptly and giving her the cold shoulder.

Poor Renee was all alone and working a menial job, while I was about to be married and receive a sizeable cash infusion.

I thought about how weird life was as I scanned the room.

Gene and Susan McDaniel had on matching buckskin vests. Though my deal with Gene hadn't panned out, we were still friendly. Lee Housekeeper, manager supreme and man of the hour was done up like Daniel Boone. Another friend of mine, Jeanne Grahme, a beautiful actress was decked out like a wood nymph. She was one of those bewitching creatures that made men's heads spin. My mother had on some long creme-colored culotte pants with matching blouse. As always, the blouse had a big bow at the neck. My mother always believed a big bow would make you look feminine while at the same time giving you the illusion of having style. It unfortunately did neither.

Even the minister — a puffed up Scientology reject — looked like a fat Wyatt Earp in his greasy long hair and string tie. All in all if you didn't know it was a wedding, it could have been a costume party. All those fancy duds were *de rigeuer* for the '60s.

That afternoon, I got married, ate little finger sandwiches, played Dylan and Hendrix L.P.'s and danced with lead-footed relatives over forty.

By the end of the day, Jaime and I had collected $1,500 bucks. Not bad for your very first wedding.

After the ceremony, Jamie was open about going back to the crib with me. His parents just smiled when we said our goodnights, his father pretending this was our first night together. Yeah, his parents knew all along, but tried, for propriety's sake, to go along with the program.

Our first night of married life was really no different than the night before we were married. Jamie stayed up, prowled around and read, while I went to bed.

Before falling asleep, I reviewed the events of the past few months. I realized, sadly, that this marriage was doomed. I felt like I was tied up without having a real commitment. On the outside, it looked like a perfect hook-up but in the inner chamber, the enclosed space of two, there was a struggle going on. Our relationship was a steamy cauldron in which a few bubbles were starting to percolate but hadn't as yet reached the surface. But soon, very soon, the pot was going to boil — boil over.

But of course, I wasn't ready to call it quits yet. Things were unfolding nicely. Why jinx it? Put the ol' whammy on something that seemed to be working.

Anyway, it was only night one.

16

GOODBYE BIG APPLE

New York was starting to feel like a claustrophobic, over-populated, dirty, potholed, roach-infested nightmare. It was no longer the exciting romantic, fast-paced, exotic, roaring metropolis I once dreamed of. My musical direction had changed and so had my imperative to be in New York. It had the wrong energy for the stuff I was into.

I'd run with the Big Dogs, been a part of the pack. Now it was time to split. To go back to California, an easy-going, sunny-dispositioned world, with enough space for trees, backyards, swimming pools, and full sized bathrooms. A place that was so laid back, folks thought 11 am was early.

L.A. wasn't the locale to sport a pale face or bar room tan. In that part of the country you had to *look* healthy even if your insides were rotting away. But now I was more than ready to lay in some big ol' backyard and rub Coppertone all over my ghostly white body. Oh yeah, I was ready to return to the very city I had been putting down for so long, because a good portion of the the Country Rock scene was situated on the West Coast.

I'd even convinced my new husband that he'd be able to better stretch out and breathe in L.A. That took some doing because he'd been in the Big Apple for less than a year. But Jamie knew what side his bread was buttered on. He was now the bass player in the new, about-to-be-world-famous, Mother Hen band. We were about to strike gold.

Yep, where the Hen went, the rooster was sure to follow!

Jamie and I decided the easiest way to make our getaway was to rent a car and and hitch up a little trailer in back. We'd haul ass across the U.S. in leisurely fashion, taking in the sights, and catching a little honeymoon time.

I thought about subletting my crib, but hell, I never wanted to set foot in the Big Apple again. Why keep a crib there? Sure, I had fulfilled a lot of my jazz fantasies there, but now other horizons were beckoning. Anyway, for some reason I felt I had hit a glass ceiling as a jazzer.

Now I was trying something else, and trying it in a new environment, one that wasn't so tight-assed and patriarchal. I'd be in good company on the the West Coast with Linda Ronstadt, Maria Muldar and Joni Mitchell. I'd heard that Joni lived in Laurel Canyon. My mother had just found a "mansion for rent" in Laurel Canyon. Now *that* was synchronicity!

Since I had lost track of most of the cats I had played with a few years ago, I thought it anticlimactic to call them up and bid them adieu. Not calling someone for a couple of years *was* like saying goodbye, wasn't it?

I had severed most of my ties, so leaving was easy.

Jamie and I set about tying up all the loose ends so we could make our getaway on schedule.

++++

Lee Housekeeper was on the line.

"It's a done deal, baby," he said smugly. "Time to sign your life away."

The lawyers had haggled over the points, worked out the kinks, and finally drawn up the contracts. I had never really been on the business end of the music business before, so I was totally blown away by all the restructuring, redefining and rewording — the inconsequential minutiae that went into drawing up a contract.

Now it was showtime!

Time for the celebratory meal and the signing of of all those onerous documents.

Alden and Harriet had planned Chinese takeout for me, Jamie, Lee Housekeeper, and the whole crew of lawyers and record execs. Dinner would be low key, informal and elegant.

All in all, there would be about eleven people at the table. Intimate but, hopefully, large in scope.

The master plan was to have a leisurely meal (leisurely because of the fumbling factor with the chopsticks), toast my good fortune, then sign on the dotted line. We projected closing the deal during dessert and coffee. A perfect ending to my New York story.

After that, Jamie and I would say our goodbyes, leap into the car with attached trailer, and we'd be off. We were planning to start the first leg of our journey before the witching hour set in.

That night, Jamie drove very cautiously to Alden and Harriet's, because of the potholes and all the baggage in the U-haul.

We arrived at my cousins' as the last few minutes of daylight disappeared.

The night was pure magic. All the old round deco street lights on Park Ave were starting to glow as the doorman held the door open. That night, the people of New York City seemed like ancient cave dwellers, inhabiting little cordoned-off cubbyholes, and inside straight-up vertical mountains. The city was a modern-day version of the New Mexico pueblos. People were *still* living on top of each other.

But soon, I'd have my own spacious dwelling place.

Leaving the Big Apple was more gratifying than arriving had been, because I was leaving *with* something. Yeah, and that something was a *substantial* something. Something I had worked my butt off for.

++++

When we got to my cousins' pad, Lee Housekeeper had already arrived. As we entered the living room, Alden and Harriet were glowing and Lee could hardly contain himself.

"We did it man. We did it!" Lee spouted. "This is just the beginning, guys. Jane, man, you look groovy. Dennis'll be creaming when he sees you."

Lee tentatively glanced sideways at my cousins. He wasn't sure that "creaming" was an acceptable word on Park Ave.

"Okay, when Dennis gets here do your thing," Lee advised me.

My *thing* was in essence to do *nothing.* Just kind of stare intensely at objects in Dennis' hand.

It had apparently worked the first time when I had gone to Dennis' office. I was actually a little intimidated because Dennis was the Vice President of R.C.A. so I kept my mouth shut and stared at the pen in his hand. Dennis was now convinced I was some kind of mystical genius that didn't have to use "mere words" to communicate.

By the time Dennis and the lawyers had arrived, washed up, and sat down to dinner, I was too hungry to talk anyway. I just stuffed my face and smiled a lot — being very careful not to smile any wider than the Mona Lisa. Besides, Alden, Harriet, and my little cousin Daren had most of the social acumen anyway. Might as well let them carry the ball.

As the contracts were being brought out and coffee was being served, Dennis arose and proposed a toast.

"To Mother Hen. The next star on the R.C.A. horizon."

"Here, here," said Housekeeper. "To the female Bob Dylan."

"To a lovely and talented young lady," Alden piped up.

Jamie and I listened as Lee explained some of the new clauses and riders that had been attached. Then the contracts were fielded over to my end of the table for signing. Alden magically appeared at my side with a new gold Parker pen. (No use signing with a crummy dimestore ballpoint.)

As I put my Jane Hancock on the document the whole table burst into applause.

Then Lee Housekeeper handed me a check for $30,000 and ten thousand in cash as Jamie had requested. Uh uh, you can't take a trip without bread.

Jamie hastily stuffed the cash in his pockets and we said our goodbyes.

"See you in a couple of weeks in California," I said to Lee as I hugged Alden, Harriet, and little Daren. "We're gonna make a fuckin' great record," I beamed.

Then Jamie, pockets bulging, spirited me out the door.

We jumped in the rent-a-car, gunned the engine, and left New York bag and baggage.

Bye Bye. So long. See ya ....

This was my shining hour. Though if you'd have asked me a few years back, I would have figured that my moment of triumph would have been playing with Miles, or getting a gig with somebody like Sonny Rollins. This was just too far out for words! But of course a journey to a different musical venue starts out one lick at a time.

++++

I glided once more through the Holland Tunnel towards a new adventure. Jamie and I sailed into the dark night, our pockets lined with cash and the car loaded down with newly acquired possessions.

I didn't give jazz, John Coltrane, Ornette Coleman, Miles Davis, Sonny Rollins, Wayne Shorter, Pony Poindexter, Bud Powell or Charlie Parker a second thought as I left the Big Apple.

And I didn't work another jazz gig, play another jazz lick, or call another tune for twenty years.

End.

www.ingramcontent.com/pod-product-compliance
Lightning Source LLC
LaVergne TN
LVHW051455080426
835509LV00017B/1766